Dutch Oven Cooking

RAY OVERTON

PHOTOGRAPHS BY
BRAD NEWTON

LONGSTREET
Atlanta, Georgia

This book is dedicated with love, admiration, and appreciation to Tyne Daly, an inspiration and influential force in my life.
Everything's coming up roses, Tyne.

Published by
LONGSTREET PRESS, INC.
A subsidiary of Cox Newspapers,
A subsidiary of Cox Enterprises, Inc.
2140 Newmarket Parkway
Suite 122
Marietta, GA 30067

Printed in The United States of America
1st printing, 1998
Library of Congress Catalog Card Number: 98-066371
ISBN: 1-56352-527-5

Electronic film prep by Advertising Technologies Incorporated, Atlanta, Georgia

Book and jacket design by Burtch Bennett Hunter

Contents

Although I have cooked with Dutch ovens at home and in my classes for years, it took a recent vacation trip to really bring home to me the amazing versatility of this essential cooking vessel. I was meeting my friends Kay, Nancy, and Jeff for two weeks of rest and relaxation at Jeff's summer house in East Hampton, New York. I arrived in Manhattan a couple of days early to meet with my literary agent and attend a couple of book signings, so I took the opportunity to buy Jeff a housewarming gift – a white 5½-quart Dutch oven.

Once Kay and I arrived in East Hampton, unpacked, and unwound with a cocktail, it was a bit late to go out for dinner. But we were famished. Fortunately, Jeff keeps a fairly well-stocked pantry. In about twenty minutes, I was able to put together a meal of scallops braised in wine over linguine using Jeff's new Dutch oven. (No matter where I go I tend to end up in the kitchen. The unwritten rule is I'll cook if you clean.)

Over the next few days, between antiquing in the village and lazing in the sun, we cooked a lot – everything from bouillabaisse to coq au vin, barbecued pork to cold poached chicken breasts, coconut fried shrimp to chicken potpie. Altogether, I think I cooked eleven or twelve times in those two weeks (didn't clean once). Almost every meal was made in Jeff's new Dutch oven.

So what *is* this remarkable utensil known as a Dutch oven? It is simply a heavy pot with a tight-fitting lid, straight or ever-so-slightly curved sides, and two sturdy handles. It can be used on top of the stove or in the oven. This style of pot has been around for hundreds of years, simmering soups over wood-burning fires or placed on the hearth, nestled in the red-hot, ash-gray coals, with a wild turkey, goose, or duck slowly roasting inside.

Every kitchen needs at least one Dutch oven. It is probably the single most-used cooking vessel in mine. In it I can braise, steam, boil, simmer, deep-fry, bake, sauté, and even marinate. The recipes in this book make use of all these techniques and will amply demonstrate the many uses of this indispensable pot.

When choosing a Dutch oven, there are several things to consider. First is material. I prefer one made with heavy cast iron. This allows the pot to absorb the heat quickly, distribute it gently and evenly, and retain the heat for maximum fuel efficiency, either over a small flame or in a low oven. The heavier the pot, the less likely you are to have "hot spots" from your stove top that can burn your food.

Dutch ovens range in size from 2 quarts all the way up to 13 quarts or even larger. I have several in varying sizes. I think $5\frac{1}{2}$ quarts is a good all-purpose size to make dishes serving up to eight people. Most of the recipes in this book call for a $5\frac{1}{2}$-quart Dutch oven, but you will also find recipes using $3\frac{1}{2}$-, $4\frac{1}{2}$-, 7-, and $8\frac{1}{2}$-quart sizes. In other words, the sizes included in these recipes are simply guidelines. Use what you have on hand. Varying the size of the Dutch oven by 1 quart either way will not make much difference, although, in this particular scenario, bigger is probably better.

Choose a Dutch oven that has a wide, flat bottom, one that makes full contact with the cooking surface. Make sure the lid fits tightly so you can simmer or braise without any loss of liquid. The handles should be easy to grasp, and the knob on the lid should be heatproof so you can use the Dutch oven on the stove top or oven. I like the inside of my Dutch oven to have an enamel finish so the pot will not absorb cooking odors or flavors. Also, an enamel coating won't react with acidic ingredients such as wine or tomatoes. Add to this wish list for the ideal pot that it be dishwasher-safe (I'm all for saving time in the clean-up) and freezer-safe. Finally, I like to serve many of my meals in the Dutch oven itself, so I want it to be attractive enough to go from stove top or oven to table. From freezer to oven to table to dishwasher – that about sums up my way of cooking in my hectic life.

Life is more complicated than it used to be. For me, trying to juggle so many different hats with writing, teaching, traveling, developing a television show, and still desiring a social life, this book exemplifies how I cook to stay sane, to entertain, and to enjoy life. I think it's how you will want to cook, too.

Soups and Stews

LAMB, BARLEY, AND MUSHROOM STEW

SERVES 8

2 tablespoons butter
2 tablespoons olive oil
3 pounds lamb shoulder, cut into 1-inch cubes
Salt and freshly ground black pepper
2 cups medium pearl barley, rinsed and drained
3 onions, thinly sliced
4 carrots, cut into ½-inch slices
3 cups thinly sliced button mushrooms

8 cups beef stock
2 cups red wine
2 tablespoons tomato paste
1 (10 ounce) package frozen English peas, defrosted
2 tablespoons chopped fresh mint
1 tablespoon chopped fresh rosemary
2 tablespoons freshly squeezed lemon juice
4 green onions, chopped

In a 5½-quart Dutch oven over medium-high heat, melt together the butter and the olive oil. Season the lamb with salt and pepper. Add the lamb to the Dutch oven and sear on all sides until it is nicely browned. Remove from the pan and set aside.

Add the barley to the Dutch oven and cook, stirring often, until the barley starts to brown and gives off a nice, nutty aroma, about 10 minutes. Do not let the barley burn or the end result will have a scorched taste.

Add the onions, carrots, and mushrooms. Cook until the mushrooms wilt, about 2 minutes. Stir in the lamb, beef stock, red wine, tomato paste, and salt and pepper to taste. Bring to a boil, reduce the heat to a simmer, cover, and cook for about 1 hour, or until the lamb and barley are tender. Add the peas, mint, and rosemary. Cook, uncovered, for 15 to 20 minutes, or until the stew is nicely thickened.

Just before serving stir in the lemon juice and adjust seasoning with additional salt and pepper. Sprinkle the stew with chopped green onions.

2

SAUTEED LEEK AND POTATO SOUP

I can't think of a better way to chase away the winter doldrums than enjoying a satisfying bowl of potato soup. Although any all-purpose potato will work, Yukon Gold offers a beautiful pale golden color and rich, buttery taste. Ground ginger and freshly grated nutmeg enhance the soul-soothing flavors of this soup.

SERVES 8

2 tablespoons olive oil

2 tablespoons butter

6 leeks, white and light green part only, rinsed and chopped

2 tablespoons chopped fresh rosemary

3½ pounds potatoes, preferably Yukon Gold, peeled and cut into 1-inch cubes

10 cups chicken stock

Salt and freshly ground black pepper

1 teaspoon ground ginger

Freshly grated nutmeg

In a 5½-quart Dutch oven melt the olive oil with the butter over medium heat. Add the leeks and rosemary and cook until the leeks are very soft but not brown, about 10 minutes. Add the potatoes, chicken stock, salt and pepper to taste, and ground ginger. Bring to a boil, reduce the heat to a simmer, partially cover, and cook for 1 hour, or until the vegetables are tender. Strain the soup and return the liquid to the Dutch oven.

Process the solids in a food processor until smooth and creamy. Return the pureed mixture to the Dutch oven and stir to combine with the broth. (For a chunky soup variation, coarsely mash the potatoes with a potato masher instead of pureeing in the food processor.) Adjust seasonings with additional salt and pepper. Ladle into bowls and top each serving with a grating of fresh nutmeg.

MADRAS CURRIED CARROT SOUP

This is an easy and elegant starter to a dinner party for family or friends. It is very pretty served in simple white soup bowls, which highlight the rich, burnt-orange color of the curry, carrots, and sweet potato. The sweet potato gives a subtle sweetness and creamy texture to the finished soup. For a lighter version, simply omit the cream.

SERVES 8 AS A STARTER

2 tablespoons olive oil
2 onions, chopped
4 garlic cloves, chopped
1 tablespoon chopped fresh rosemary
2 tablespoons mild curry powder,
   preferably Madras
1 tart apple, such as Granny Smith, peeled,
   cored, and cut into chunks

1 sweet potato, peeled and cut into chunks
2 pounds baby carrots, scraped
8 cups chicken stock
1 tablespoon red wine vinegar
1 tablespoon Worcestershire sauce
1 tablespoon sugar
Salt and freshly ground black pepper
1 cup heavy cream
Fresh chives, tied in bundles or chopped

In a 5½-quart Dutch oven heat the olive oil over medium heat until sizzling. Add the onions and garlic and cook, stirring constantly, until the onions just begin to brown, about 5 minutes. Add the rosemary and curry powder and cook for 3 minutes. Stir in the chopped apple, sweet potato, and baby carrots. Add the chicken stock and bring to a boil.

Reduce the heat to a simmer, cover, and cook for 30 minutes, stirring occasionally. Stir in the red wine vinegar, Worcestershire sauce, sugar, and salt and pepper to taste.

Strain the soup and return the liquid to the Dutch oven. Process the solids in a food processor until smooth. Add the pureed mixture back to the Dutch oven. (The soup freezes very well at this point. When ready to serve, defrost and heat in the Dutch oven, then continue with the recipe.)

Add the cream and heat until the mixture just begins to simmer. Serve with the chive bundles or freshly chopped chives sprinkled on top.

4

CHICKEN MINESTRONE SOUP

In Italian , minestrone literally translated means "big soup." The key ingredients in this thick whole-meal soup include pasta, fresh vegetables, beans, and a heavy topping of freshly grated cheese.

SERVES 8 TO 10

¼ cup olive oil

4 garlic cloves, chopped

3 carrots, diced

3 onions, diced

4 ribs of celery, thinly sliced

4 green onions, chopped

10 cups chicken stock

4 boneless, skinless chicken breasts

1 bay leaf, crumbled

1 (10 ounce) package frozen French-cut green beans, or 1 cup green beans cut into 1-inch pieces

1 teaspoon salt

1 teaspoon black pepper

1 (15½ ounce) can northern white beans, rinsed and drained

1 (15½ ounce) can red kidney beans, rinsed and drained

1 (15½ ounce) can chickpeas, rinsed and drained

1 cup cauliflower florets

1 cup macaroni or small shell-shaped pasta

1 zucchini, cut in half lengthwise and sliced crosswise in ¼-inch crescents

1 yellow squash, cut in half lengthwise and sliced crosswise in ¼-inch crescents

1 (15½ ounce) can diced tomatoes with juice

½ cup chopped fresh basil, or ⅓ cup commercial pesto sauce

2 cups freshly grated Parmesan or Romano cheese

In an 8½-quart Dutch oven heat the olive oil over medium-high heat and add the garlic, carrots, onions, celery, and green onions. Cook until the vegetables are lightly browned, about 15 minutes.

Add the chicken stock, chicken breasts, and crumbled bay leaf. Bring to a boil. Reduce the heat to a simmer and cook, covered, for 20 minutes. Remove from the heat. Remove the chicken and shred with forks or cut into ¾-inch pieces. Set aside.

Return the Dutch oven to the heat and add the green beans, salt, pepper, white beans, kidney beans, chickpeas, cauliflower, and pasta. Cook, covered, over medium heat until pasta is tender, about 8 to 10 minutes. Add the zucchini, yellow squash, diced tomatoes, and reserved chicken. Cook, uncovered, for 3 minutes.

Stir in the basil or pesto sauce and ladle the soup into individual serving bowls. Sprinkle each bowl with a generous topping of grated cheese. Serve at once.

SOUPS AND STEWS

BRUNSWICK STEW

Debate continues as to whether this stew originated in Brunswick, Georgia, or Brunswick, Virginia. It doesn't matter to me— I'm just glad it has been passed down from generation to generation. This recipe makes a gracious plenty but it will freeze very well. It's not complicated at all; basically the hardest part is having to wait while it slowly simmers. Brunswick Stew is perfect on its own, served with hush puppies, or as a starter to a big barbeque celebration.

SERVES 14 TO 16

1 (4 pound) chicken
2½ quarts water
4 carrots, shredded
6 ribs of celery, thinly sliced
Salt and freshly ground black pepper
3 onions, chopped
1 pound new potatoes, diced
3 pounds chuck roast, cut into 2-inch cubes
8 slices of bacon, chopped
2 (28 ounce) cans chopped tomatoes with added puree

1 (16 ounce) bag frozen white corn, defrosted
1 (16 ounce) bag frozen lima beans, defrosted
1 (16 ounce) bag frozen sliced okra, defrosted
2 tablespoons Worcestershire sauce
1 tablespoon sugar
½ cup chopped flat-leaf parsley
1 teaspoon celery seeds
1 teaspoon turmeric
Apple cider vinegar to taste
Tabasco to taste

In an 8½-quart Dutch oven combine the chicken, water, carrots, celery, and salt and pepper. Bring to a boil, skim the surface for any scum that rises to the top, reduce the heat to a simmer, cover, and cook for 1 hour. Remove from the heat and allow the chicken to cool in the broth. Remove the chicken from the broth and separate the skin and bones from the meat. Discard the skin and bones and coarsely chop the chicken meat.

Remove the fat that has risen to the top of the broth and return the chicken to the broth. Add the onions, diced potatoes, chuck roast, bacon, and tomatoes. Bring to a boil, reduce the heat to a simmer, and cook, covered, over low heat for 3 hours, stirring occasionally.

Stir in the corn, lima beans, okra, Worcestershire sauce, sugar, parsley, celery seed, turmeric, and a generous amount of salt and pepper to taste. Cook over low heat, uncovered, for 1 hour, or until the stew is very thick and flavorful. (You should almost be able to eat it with a fork.)

Ladle the stew into bowls and drizzle each serving with a small amount of apple cider vinegar and a dash of Tabasco.

SOUTHWESTERN BEEF STEW WITH BARLEY

SERVES 8

3 tablespoons peanut oil
1 (4 pound) chuck roast, trimmed of visible
  fat and cut into 2-inch chunks
Salt and freshly ground black pepper
3 onions, chopped
6 garlic cloves, chopped
2 chopped chipotle peppers in adobo sauce
  or 2 jalapeño peppers, seeded and chopped
4 carrots, cut into 1-inch chunks
2 cups sliced button mushrooms
1 large jicama or 2 sweet potatoes, peeled
  and cut into 1-inch chunks
2 (10½ ounce) cans chopped tomatoes
  with diced chiles, such as Rotel

1 (16 ounce) can tomato sauce
1 (8 ounce) can enchilada sauce
2 cups water
2 tablespoons chili powder
1 tablespoon ground cumin
1 (1 ounce) square unsweetened chocolate,
  chopped
½ cup chopped fresh cilantro
Juice of 2 limes
1 teaspoon sugar
⅔ cup medium pearl barley, rinsed and drained
1 (12 ounce) bottle Mexican beer or 1½ cups
  beef stock
Sour cream
Lime wedges

In a 5½-quart Dutch oven heat the peanut oil over medium-high heat until sizzling. Lightly season the chuck roast with salt and pepper. Place the meat in the Dutch oven and cook until the meat is browned on all sides. Remove from the pan and set aside.

To the drippings in the pan, add the onion, garlic, chipotles or jalapeño peppers, carrots, mushrooms, and jicama or sweet potato. Cook the vegetables over medium heat until they begin to brown, about 20 minutes. Return the meat to the pan.

Stir in the tomatoes with chiles, tomato sauce, enchilada sauce, water, chili powder, cumin, unsweetened chocolate, cilantro, lime juice, and sugar. Simmer over low heat, covered, for 1½ hours. Be sure to stir the stew every now and then to prevent sticking.

Stir in the rinsed barley and the beer. Return to a boil, reduce the heat to medium-low and cook, uncovered, stirring occasionally, for 30 to 45 minutes, or until the barley is tender and the vegetable mixture is thick and luscious. Season to taste with additional salt and pepper. Serve in bowls, with dollops of sour cream and lime wedges.

8

NAVY BEAN SOUP

You can substitute a 16-ounce box of 5-, 7-, or 13-bean mix for the navy beans in this recipe. These prepackaged varieties are sold in most supermarkets today.

SERVES 8 TO 10

16 ounces dried navy (pea) beans, picked over

6 slices thick, country-style peppered bacon, chopped

4 onions, thinly sliced

4 garlic cloves, thinly sliced

10 cups chicken stock

1 tablespoon chopped fresh oregano

1 tablespoon chopped fresh rosemary

1 bay leaf, crumbled

Salt and freshly ground black pepper

½ teaspoon red pepper flakes

1 pound baby carrots, scraped

4 ribs of celery, thinly sliced

½ cup heavy cream

3 tablespoons chopped fresh basil

The night before: Place the dried beans in a large bowl and cover with water by 3 inches. Soak the beans overnight and drain in a colander. Set aside until ready to use.

In a 5½-quart Dutch oven cook the bacon over medium-high heat until some of the fat is rendered, about 2 minutes. Add the onions and garlic. Cook until they just begin to brown, about 10 to 15 minutes.

Add the chicken stock, oregano, rosemary, and bay leaf. Bring to a boil. Add the soaked and drained beans, salt and pepper to taste, and red pepper flakes. Cover, reduce the heat to a simmer, and cook for 1 hour.

Stir in the carrots and celery. Cook, covered, until the vegetables and navy beans are very tender, about 1½ hours. Remove 3 cups of the solids from the Dutch oven and puree in a food processor until smooth. Return the pureed solids to the soup, along with the cream. Stir until just heated through.

Add the basil and adjust seasonings with additional salt and pepper. Serve at once.

HEARTY BEEF CHILI

This is my favorite chili. It is the perfect food for Saturday afternoon football watching, lunch after mountain hiking or snow skiing, or a casual supper for a tree trimming or holiday caroling party. The chili freezes well for about 3 months, so I usually keep a batch on hand. It is especially good served piping hot and ladled over crumbled jalapeño corn bread.

SERVES 10 TO 12

¼ cup vegetable oil
1 (3½ pound) chuck roast, cut into 1-inch cubes
2 pounds lean ground chuck
4 onions, chopped
6 garlic cloves, chopped
2 (28 ounce) cans chopped tomatoes with their juice
2 (4 ounce) cans chopped mild green chiles, rinsed and drained
1 (12 ounce) bottle dark beer mixed with 1 (6 ounce) can tomato paste

1 cup beef stock
¼ cup red wine vinegar
¼ cup chili powder
2 tablespoons ground cumin
½ to 1 teaspoon red pepper flakes
Salt and freshly ground black pepper
3 (15½ ounce) cans light kidney beans, rinsed and drained
1 (15½ ounce) can black beans, rinsed and drained
⅓ cup chopped fresh cilantro

In an 8½-quart Dutch oven heat the oil over medium-high heat. Add the beef cubes and ground chuck. Stir until the meat is cooked through and well browned on all sides. Remove the meat from the pan and set aside. Discard all but ¼ cup of the drippings.

Add the onions and garlic and sauté over medium-high heat until soft, about 5 to 7 minutes. Add the chopped tomatoes, chiles, beer mixed with tomato paste, beef stock, red wine vinegar, chili powder, cumin, red pepper flakes, and salt and pepper to taste. Reduce the heat to low and simmer, uncovered, for about 1 hour, or until nicely thickened.

Stir in the kidney beans, black beans, and the reserved meat and simmer, uncovered, for another hour, stirring often to prevent sticking. Stir in the cilantro. Taste and adjust seasoning with additional salt and pepper. Serve at once.

10

TEX-MEX VEGETARIAN CHILI

Virtually the only fat in this recipe is 1 tablespoon of vegetable oil used for sautéeing. I guarantee you won't even miss the fat in this full-flavored Southwestern concoction.

SERVES 8 TO 10

1 tablespoon vegetable oil
4 onions, chopped
6 garlic cloves, chopped
3 carrots, chopped
2 red bell peppers, seeded and chopped
2 green bell peppers, seeded and chopped
1 (28 ounce) can chopped tomatoes with juice
2 (4 ounce) cans chopped mild green chiles, drained
1 (12 ounce) bottle light beer mixed with 1 (6 ounce) can tomato paste

1½ cups bulgur, soaked for 20 minutes in 3 cups boiling vegetable stock
1 (15½ ounce) can light kidney beans, rinsed and drained
1 (15½ ounce) can black beans, rinsed and drained
1 (15½ ounce) can whole kernel corn, rinsed and drained
¼ cup red wine vinegar
2 tablespoons chili powder
1 tablespoon ground cumin
½ teaspoon red pepper flakes
Salt and freshly ground black pepper

Heat the oil in a 5½-quart Dutch oven over medium-high heat. Add the onions, garlic, carrots, red pepper, and green pepper. Cook until the vegetables are soft and begin to caramelize, about 15 minutes. Add the chopped tomatoes, chiles, beer mixed with tomato paste, bulgur with vegetable stock, kidney beans, black beans, corn, red wine vinegar, chili powder, cumin, red pepper flakes, and salt and pepper to taste. Reduce the heat to low and simmer, uncovered, stirring occasionally, for 1 hour, or until nicely thickened.

CHICKEN AND WHITE BEAN CHILI

This chili is as thick and delicious as any hearty beef-and-bean variety, but it is much lower in fat than the traditional version. It freezes very well, so I usually make the entire recipe and freeze the remainder in single-serving batches for busy week nights when I'm too tired to cook.

SERVES 8 TO 10

2 tablespoons olive oil
4 onions, chopped
6 garlic cloves, chopped
4 (4 ounce) cans chopped mild green chiles, drained
1 (12 ounce) bottle of regular (not dark) beer
2 cups chicken stock
3 tablespoons chili powder
2 tablespoons ground cumin
½ teaspoon red pepper flakes
Salt and freshly ground black pepper
6 boneless, skinless chicken thighs, cut into 1-inch cubes

2 (15½ ounce) cans white northern beans, rinsed and drained
1 (15½ ounce) can chickpeas, rinsed and drained
1 (15½ ounce) can cream-style corn
¼ cup chopped fresh cilantro
¼ cup lime juice

OPTIONAL TOPPINGS

Grated cheddar and Monterey Jack cheeses
Sour cream
Chopped green onions
Chopped tomatoes
Sliced jalapeño peppers
Tortilla chips

Lightly coat a 5½-quart Dutch oven with nonstick cooking spray. Over medium-high heat, add the olive oil, onions, and garlic and cook until soft, about 7 minutes. Add the chopped green chiles, beer, chicken stock, chili powder, cumin, red pepper flakes, and salt and pepper to taste. Stir in the chicken. Reduce the heat to low and simmer, covered, for about 45 minutes, or until the mixture is nicely thickened and the chicken is cooked.

Stir in the northern beans, chickpeas, and creamed corn. Simmer, uncovered, for 20 minutes, stirring often to prevent sticking. Stir in the chopped cilantro and lime juice and mix very well. Serve in large bowls, garnished with the optional toppings if desired.

GEORGIA BOUILLABAISSE

Authentic bouillabaisse is an ocean away, but substituting some very Southern staples like Vidalia onions, catfish, shrimp, and crab transforms this Provençal fisherman's stew into a down-home delight. The ingredient list may seem daunting, but every ingredient is essential to create a dish that is the apotheosis of what I call peasant chic.

SERVES 8 TO 10

3 tablespoons olive oil

3 Vidalia onions, thinly sliced

2 carrots, shredded

3 leeks, white and light green part only, rinsed and chopped

2 fennel bulbs, halved, core removed, and thinly sliced

4 garlic cloves, chopped

1 (28 ounce) can chopped tomatoes with their juice

8 cups fish stock or a combination of 4 cups chicken stock mixed with 4 cups clam juice

1 cup dry white wine

Salt and freshly ground black pepper

1 pound catfish fillets, cut into 1-inch chunks

½ pound large shrimp, peeled and deveined

½ pound lump crab meat, picked over for shells

1 pound mussels, scrubbed, rinsed well, and beards removed

1 tablespoon freshly squeezed lemon juice

½ teaspoon saffron threads

½ cup chopped flat-leaf parsley

1 tablespoon fresh thyme leaves

2 tablespoons chopped fresh tarragon

1 teaspoon grated orange zest

Rouille Sauce (recipe follows)

Rosemary Garlic Croutons (recipe follows)

In an 8½-quart Dutch oven over medium-high heat, heat the olive oil. Add the Vidalia onions, carrots, leeks, fennel, and garlic. Cook until the vegetables are soft, about 10 minutes. Add the chopped tomatoes, fish stock, white wine, and salt and pepper to taste. Bring to a boil, cover, and reduce the heat to a simmer. Cook for 45 minutes, stirring occasionally.

Stir in the catfish, shrimp, crab meat, and mussels. Cover and cook for 5 minutes, or until the fish is white and opaque, the shrimp are pink and curled, and the mussels have opened. Discard any mussels that do not open.

In a small bowl mix together the lemon juice and saffron. Stir into the bouillabaisse, along with the parsley, thyme, tarragon, and orange zest. Simmer for 2 minutes more. Adjust the seasonings with additional salt and pepper. Ladle into shallow soup bowls, top with Rouille Sauce and Rosemary Garlic Croutons, and serve at once.

14

ROUILLE SAUCE

MAKES 1½ CUPS

½ cup seasoned bread crumbs
¼ teaspoon saffron threads
Pinch of cayenne pepper
Juice of 2 lemons
¼ cup egg substitute, chilled
3 garlic cloves, peeled
¾ cup extra-virgin olive oil
1 red bell pepper, roasted, peeled, seeded, and thinly sliced
Salt and freshly ground black pepper

In a small bowl combine the bread crumbs with the saffron threads, cayenne pepper, and lemon juice. Let mixture soak for 15 minutes. Transfer to a food processor. Add the egg substitute and garlic and process until smooth. While the machine is running, slowly add the olive oil in a thin, steady stream, until the mixture becomes thickened and emulsified. Add the roasted red bell pepper and salt and pepper to taste. Process until the pepper is coarsely chopped.

ROSEMARY GARLIC CROUTONS

MAKES ABOUT 3 CUPS

⅓ cup extra-virgin olive oil
2 garlic cloves, very finely chopped
2 tablespoons chopped fresh rosemary
½ cup freshly grated Parmesan cheese
Salt and freshly ground black pepper
12 to 14 thin slices day-old French baguette, cut into cubes

Preheat the oven to 375°F. In a large bowl combine the olive oil, garlic, rosemary, Parmesan cheese, and salt and pepper to taste. Add the bread cubes and toss to evenly coat. Spread on a large, parchment-lined baking sheet. Bake for 12 to 15 minutes, or until the croutons are crisp and lightly browned. Croutons can be stored in an airtight container for 4 to 5 days, or frozen for up to 1 month.

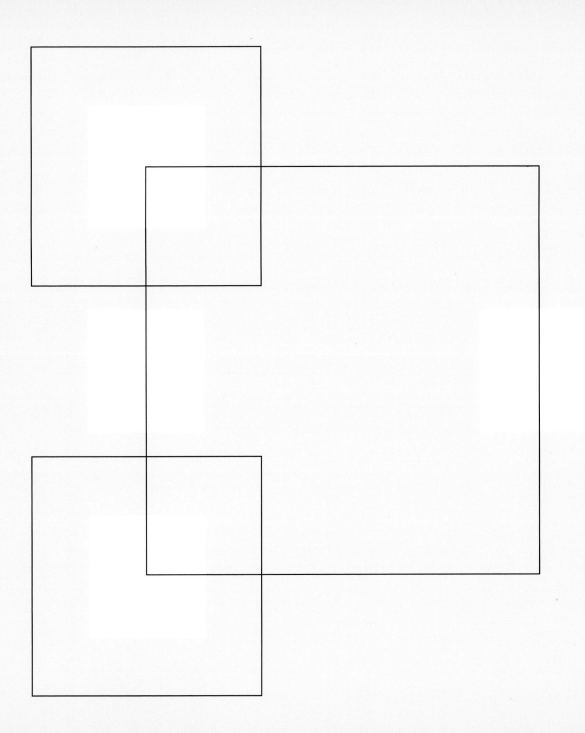

Mostly Vegetable

SUN-DRIED TOMATO AND PESTO RISOTTO

CONFETTI VEGETABLE HASH

BAKED BEANS, BOSTON STYLE, WITH STEAMED BROWN BREAD

CARIBBEAN COUSCOUS WITH SAUTEED GRATED SWEET POTATOES

VEGETABLE TEMPURA

MEDITERRANEAN RATATOUILLE

LENTIL, FENNEL, PARSLEY, AND GOAT CHEESE SALAD

HOPPIN' JOHN WITH TOMATILLOS AND CHIPOTLES

NEW ORLEANS RED BEANS AND RICE

BULGUR PILAF

SAFFRON-INFUSED COUSCOUS WITH VEGETABLES
AND DRIED CRANBERRIES

ROOT VEGETABLE GRATIN

SUN-DRIED TOMATO AND PESTO RISOTTO

To toast the pine nuts, place them on a baking sheet in a preheated 350°F oven for 6 to 8 minutes.

SERVES 6

8 cups chicken stock or vegetable stock
½ teaspoon fennel seeds, slightly crushed
2 tablespoons olive oil
2 onions, chopped
3 garlic cloves, chopped
2 carrots, shredded
3 cups Arborio rice
Grated zest of 2 lemons
Juice of 2 lemons

⅔ cup cream
1 cup oil-packed sun-dried tomatoes, drained and coarsely chopped
⅓ cup commercial pesto sauce
½ cup pitted black olives
2 tablespoons capers, rinsed and drained
1 cup freshly grated Parmesan cheese, divided
Freshly ground black pepper
½ cup lightly toasted pine nuts

In a 2½-quart saucepan, bring the stock and fennel seeds to a boil. Lower the heat and maintain the stock at a simmer.

In a 4½-quart Dutch oven heat the olive oil over medium high-heat. Add the onions, garlic, and shredded carrots. Cook until soft and just beginning to wilt, about 2 to 3 minutes. Add the Arborio rice and cook, stirring with a wooden spoon, until the grains are well coated, about 2 minutes. Add the lemon zest and the juice and mix well.

Add the simmering stock, ½ cup at a time, to the rice, stirring frequently. Let the rice completely absorb the stock before adding any more liquid. Continue stirring, adding the stock ½ cup at a time, until all the stock has been used. This whole process should take about 20 minutes.

Add the cream and stir until it is nearly absorbed. Stir in the sun-dried tomatoes, pesto, black olives, capers, and ½ cup of the Parmesan cheese. Cover and let sit for 5 minutes.

Transfer to a serving dish and sprinkle with the remaining ½ cup Parmesan cheese and freshly ground black pepper to taste. Top with the pine nuts. Serve at once.

18

CONFETTI VEGETABLE HASH

I enjoy this colorful dish of sautéed vegetables topped with poached eggs for Sunday brunch, or as a side dish paired with a juicy, pan-seared steak or fish fillet. For an interesting salad, slightly undercook the vegetables, then toss them with a simple vinaigrette while they are still warm. Let the vegetables marinate in the dressing for a couple of hours. Serve chilled or at room temperature for your next outdoor gathering.

SERVES 4 AS AN ENTREE, 8 AS A SIDE DISH

3 tablespoons olive oil

⅓ cup butter

4 large russet potatoes, scrubbed and cut into ½-inch dice (do not peel)

2 sweet potatoes, peeled and cut into ½-inch dice

1 green bell pepper, seeded and chopped

1 red bell pepper, seeded and chopped

2 red onions, chopped

4 garlic cloves, chopped

6 green onions, chopped

2 cups sliced button mushrooms

6 plum tomatoes, seeded and diced

Salt and freshly ground black pepper

½ teaspoon red pepper flakes (or to taste)

2 tablespoons chopped fresh oregano

½ cup chopped fresh parsley

1 cup freshly grated Parmesan cheese

In a 5½-quart Dutch oven set over medium heat, melt together the olive oil and butter. Add the potatoes, sweet potatoes, green bell pepper, red bell pepper, red onions, and garlic. Cook over medium heat, stirring often to prevent sticking, until potatoes are tender and lightly browned, about 35 to 40 minutes.

Add the green onions, mushrooms, and plum tomatoes. Cook for 5 to 10 minutes, or until the mushrooms just begin to wilt. Season to taste with salt and pepper. Stir in the red pepper flakes, oregano, and parsley. Sprinkle with the grated Parmesan cheese just before serving. Serve warm or at room temperature.

BAKED BEANS, BOSTON STYLE, WITH STEAMED BROWN BREAD

I love the zing that freshly chopped ginger and horseradish add to this traditional bean pot. Served with Steamed Brown Bread, these beans make a hearty meal on their own. They are also an excellent side dish that pairs nicely with just about anything from a simple campfire cookout to a casual fish fry.

SERVES 6 TO 8 AS AN ENTREE, 10 TO 12 AS A SIDE DISH

4 cups dried navy or white beans
½ pound bacon, cut into 1-inch pieces
4 onions, thinly sliced
8 garlic cloves, thinly sliced
2 tablespoons chopped ginger
⅔ cup brown sugar

1 cup dark molasses
¼ cup Dijon-style mustard
1 tablespoon dry mustard
3 tablespoons prepared horseradish
2 cups chili sauce or tomato sauce
Salt and freshly ground black pepper
About 3 quarts beef stock or water

The night before: Spread the beans out on a baking sheet and pick through to remove any small stones or debris. Place the beans in a colander and rinse under cold running water for 1 minute. Transfer the beans to a 5½-quart Dutch oven, add enough water to cover them by 3 inches, and soak the beans overnight. Drain. (Alternately, place the beans in the Dutch oven with enough water to cover, bring them to a full, rolling boil, cover, and turn off the heat. Let the beans soak for 1 hour. Drain the beans in a colander and set aside.)

Preheat the oven to 325°F. In a 5½-quart Dutch oven combine the bacon, onions, garlic, and ginger. Cook over medium-high heat until the bacon has lightly browned and the onions are wilted, about 10 minutes. Add the drained beans, brown sugar, molasses, Dijon mustard, dry mustard, horseradish, chili sauce or tomato sauce, and salt and pepper to taste. Stir to mix well. Add enough beef stock or water to just cover the beans. Cover the pot and place in the oven. Cook for 4 hours. Stir every hour and check the stock level, adding more as needed.

Remove the lid and continue baking (adding more stock or water to keep the beans moist) for 2 hours longer, or until the beans are tender and the color of deep caramel. Cover and let the beans sit for 15 minutes before serving with Steamed Brown Bread (recipe follows).

20

STEAMED BROWN BREAD

MAKES 1 LOAF

¼ cup cornmeal (not cornmeal mix)
½ cup rye flour
¼ cup all-purpose flour
½ cup whole-wheat flour

1 teaspoon baking soda
½ teaspoon baking powder
½ teaspoon salt
½ cup dark molasses
1 cup buttermilk

Grease and flour a clean 1-pound coffee container, line the bottom with a disk of wax paper, and grease and flour the paper. Set aside.

In a large bowl sift together the cornmeal, rye flour, all-purpose flour, whole-wheat flour, baking soda, baking powder, and salt. In a smaller bowl, whisk together the dark molasses and the buttermilk. Slowly pour the liquid ingredients into the bowl containing the flours. Stir just enough to blend the ingredients. Do not overmix. Pour the batter in the prepared coffee can. Double a piece of aluminum foil, lightly butter one side, and place the foil, buttered side down, over the can. Tie the foil securely in place with kitchen twine.

Place a tea towel or round cooling rack in the bottom of an 8½-quart Dutch oven or stock pot with a tight-fitting lid. Place the coffee can on top of the tea towel or round cooling rack and fill the pot with enough hot water to come halfway up the sides of the can. Cover the pot with the lid. Bring the water to a simmer and cook or steam the bread for 1½ to 2 hours, or until a wooden skewer inserted into the bread comes out clean. The bread should no longer be sticky and should spring back when slightly pressed. (It may be necessary to add more hot water during the steaming time. You want to maintain a level of water halfway up the side of the can.)

Transfer the coffee can to a wire rack and allow to cool for a few minutes. Carefully remove the bread from the can and allow it to cool on its side. For easier slicing and more uniform pieces, slice the bread with a serrated knife.

CARIBBEAN COUSCOUS WITH SAUTEED GRATED SWEET POTATOES

With its tastes and textures from around the world, this dish exemplifies the global kitchen philosophy that pervades so much of my cooking today. In recent years this couscous has become a welcome addition to my family's holiday dinners.

SERVES 4 TO 6 AS AN ENTREE, 8 TO 10 AS A SIDE DISH

8 tablespoons (1 stick) butter
4 sweet potatoes, peeled and coarsely grated
8 green onions, chopped
1 cup sliced button mushrooms
1 jalapeño pepper, seeded and finely chopped
½ teaspoon allspice
2 teaspoons poultry seasoning
2 teaspoons cumin powder
Juice of 2 oranges

Grated zest of 2 oranges
7 cups chicken stock
1½ cups assorted chopped dried fruit, such as apples, pears, apricots, peaches, raisins, and dried cranberries
¾ cup shredded sweetened coconut
3 cups couscous
Salt and freshly ground black pepper
1 cup chopped toasted pecans
¼ cup chopped fresh cilantro

In a 5½-quart Dutch oven melt the butter over medium heat. Add the grated sweet potatoes and cook, stirring until almost cooked through, about 20 minutes. Stir in the green onions, mushrooms, jalapeño pepper, allspice, poultry seasoning, cumin, orange juice, and orange zest.

Add the chicken stock to the Dutch oven and bring to a boil. Cover and simmer for 5 minutes. Stir in the dried fruit, coconut, and couscous. Remove from the heat, cover, and let sit for 5 minutes. Remove the cover, fluff the couscous with a fork, season to taste with salt and pepper, and stir in the toasted pecans and cilantro. Transfer the couscous to a large serving bowl and serve at once.

VEGETABLE TEMPURA

The secret to a good tempura is a light batter that fries to a golden crisp. To achieve this, do not overmix the batter ingredients, and be sure the oil is hot enough before frying to prevent the vegetables from absorbing too much oil.

SERVES 8 TO 10 AS AN APPETIZER

VEGETABLES (ANY ASSORTMENT BELOW WORKS NICELY)

1 small head broccoli, separated into florets

1 zucchini, halved lengthwise and cut into 3-inch sticks

1 bunch green onions, trimmed and cut into 3-inch lengths

1 bunch pencil-thin asparagus, woody stems removed, cut into 3-inch lengths

8 ounces shiitake mushrooms, woody stems discarded, caps left whole

1 sweet potato, peeled and cut crosswise into ¼-inch slices

2 carrots, cut into 3-inch sticks

DIPPING SAUCE

1 cup light soy sauce

½ cup sake or rice wine vinegar

3 tablespoons dark Asian sesame oil

2 tablespoons hot Chinese mustard

2 tablespoons chopped ginger

1 tablespoon Chinese chili garlic sauce

3 green onions, chopped

BATTER

4 cups all-purpose flour, divided

Salt and freshly ground black pepper

Cayenne pepper

2 eggs, lightly beaten

2 cups cold sparkling water

About 8 cups peanut oil for deep-frying

In a small bowl slowly whisk together the soy sauce, sake, sesame oil, Chinese mustard, ginger, chili garlic sauce, and chopped green onions. Set aside.

Prepare the vegetables as directed above and place in individual bowls.

In a shallow pie plate mix together 1½ cups of the all-purpose flour, and a pinch of salt, pepper, and cayenne pepper.

In a large bowl whisk together the eggs and sparkling water. Sift the remaining 2½ cups flour into the bowl and lightly whisk until just combined. (The batter should be slightly lumpy. If it is overmixed it will become heavy when it is deep-fried.) Transfer the batter to a large, shallow dish.

24

Preheat the oven to 200°F. In a 5½-quart Dutch oven heat the peanut oil until the temperature registers 365°F. (A cube of bread should brown in the hot oil in about 30 to 45 seconds.)

Line several baking sheets with paper towels. Dredge the broccoli florets in the seasoned flour, then place them in the batter. Using tongs, carefully lift out the florets and let the excess batter drip off before gently placing in the hot oil. Deep-fry the broccoli until crisp, turning once during cooking, about 1 to 2 minutes. With a slotted spoon, transfer the broccoli to the prepared baking sheets and place in the oven to keep warm. Do not cover or crowd the vegetables or they will get soggy.

Repeat with the remaining vegetables, deep-frying the zucchini, green onions, asparagus, and mushrooms for about 1 to 2 minutes and the sweet potato and carrots for about 2 to 3 minutes. Drain and keep warm in the oven as directed above. When all the vegetables are cooked, arrange on a large serving platter and lightly season with salt and pepper. Transfer the dipping sauce to a serving bowl and serve at once.

MEDITERRANEAN RATATOUILLE

Ratatouille is wonderful as a side dish with pasta, or as a bed for grilled lamb, pork, beef, or chicken. This also makes an excellent appetizer dip, served with toasted pita wedges or Belgian endive spears. For crostini, place 2 to 3 tablespoons of the ratatouille on sliced day-old French bread, top with grated Parmesan cheese, and run the crostini under the broiler for a couple of minutes.

SERVES 4 TO 6 AS AN ENTREE, 8 TO 10 AS A SIDE DISH

1 large eggplant, cut into ½-inch slices and lightly scored with a knife
Kosher salt
2 zucchini, cut into ½-inch slices
½ cup olive oil, divided
4 onions, thinly sliced
2 red bell peppers, seeded and thinly sliced
2 green bell peppers, seeded and thinly sliced
6 garlic cloves, chopped
½ cup balsamic vinegar
1 (28 ounce) can plum tomatoes, coarsely chopped, with their juice
1 cup assorted chopped fresh herbs such as thyme, basil, parsley, oregano, and rosemary, divided
1 to 2 teaspoons sugar
1 teaspoon salt
Freshly ground black pepper

Preheat the oven to 375°F. Place the eggplant in a colander and sprinkle with the kosher salt. Leave for 30 minutes. Rinse, drain, and pat the eggplant dry. Brush the eggplant and zucchini slices with all but 2 tablespoons of the olive oil. Place on a lightly oiled baking sheet. Bake in the oven for 30 minutes, or until soft and just beginning to brown. Set aside to cool.

In a 5½-quart Dutch oven heat the remaining oil over medium-high heat. Add the onions, red and green bell peppers, and garlic. Cook until soft, about 8 to 10 minutes.

Add the baked eggplant and the zucchini, balsamic vinegar, tomatoes, ½ cup of the herbs, sugar, salt and freshly ground black pepper to taste. Simmer, uncovered, for 1 hour. Stir occasionally to prevent sticking. Add the remaining ½ cup of herbs and cook for 15 minutes more. Season to taste with salt and pepper. Serve hot or at room temperature.

26

LENTIL, FENNEL, PARSLEY, AND GOAT CHEESE SALAD

One of my favorite menus is this main-course vegetarian salad with crispy bread sticks and a chilled Riesling from Alsace. Stilton cheese and pears drizzled with honey and toasted walnuts complete the meal.

SERVES 8

1 onion, chopped
8 garlic cloves, chopped, divided
2 ribs of celery, chopped
2 carrots, coarsely grated
2 tablespoons chopped fresh rosemary
3 cups green or brown lentils, rinsed and picked over
8 cups chicken stock
2 bay leaves, crumbled (stems removed)
Salt and freshly ground black pepper

Juice of 3 lemons
1 tablespoon ground cumin
2 tablespoon Dijon-style mustard
Sugar to taste
⅓ cup extra-virgin olive oil
1 cup chopped fresh parsley
2 fennel bulbs, cored and thinly sliced
6 ounces feta cheese, crumbled
2 cups croutons
1 cup pitted Greek black olives, such as kalamata

In a 4½-quart Dutch oven combine the onion, half of the chopped garlic, celery, carrots, rosemary, lentils, chicken stock, and bay leaves. Bring to a boil, reduce the heat to a simmer, cover, and cook 30 to 40 minutes, or until the lentils are tender. (Do not overcook the lentils or they will become mushy.) Drain the lentils and transfer to a large bowl to cool. Season to taste with salt and pepper. Meanwhile, make the vinaigrette: In a small bowl, whisk together the lemon juice, cumin, Dijon mustard, the remaining chopped garlic, and salt, pepper, and sugar to taste. Continue to whisk as you add the olive oil in a thin, steady stream until the dressing is thick and emulsified. Set aside.

Stir the parsley and fennel into the cooled lentil mixture. Drizzle with the vinaigrette and toss to coat. Cover and refrigerate for at least 2 hours. Just before serving, toss once more and top with feta cheese, croutons, and black olives.

HOPPIN' JOHN WITH TOMATILLOS AND CHIPOTLES

I have given this traditional Southern classic a decidedly Southwestern flavor with the addition of chipotles, tomatillos, chili powder, cilantro, and lime juice. This hearty rice and bean combination makes a wonderful vegetarian supper or a delicious accompaniment to grilled chicken, beef, or pork.

SERVES 4 TO 6 AS AN ENTREE, 8 TO 10 AS A SIDE DISH

2 tablespoons peanut oil

2 red onions, chopped

3 carrots, shredded

4 garlic cloves, chopped

3 dried chipotle peppers, reconstituted, seeded and chopped (see note)

3 cups uncooked long-grain white rice

8 cups chicken stock

1 tablespoon chili powder

2 teaspoons ground cumin

½ teaspoon allspice

Salt and freshly ground black pepper

1 (16 ounce) bag frozen black-eyed peas, defrosted

1 (28 ounce) can diced tomatoes with their juice

12 tomatillos, husks removed, rinsed, and cut into quarters

Juice of 1 lime

4 green onions, chopped

½ cup chopped fresh cilantro

Preheat the oven to 350°F. In a 5½-quart Dutch oven over medium-high heat, heat the peanut oil until sizzling hot. Add the red onions and carrots and cook for 5 minutes, or until the onions begin to wilt slightly. Stir in the garlic, chipotle peppers, and rice. Cook for 2 minutes, or until the rice is slightly puffed and opaque.

Stir in the chicken stock, chili powder, cumin, allspice, and salt and pepper to taste. Bring to a boil, then add the black-eyed peas, tomatoes, and tomatillos. Cover and bake for 1 hour, or until the rice is tender and most of the liquid has been absorbed. Remove from the oven and allow to rest for 10 minutes. Stir in the lime juice, green onions, and cilantro. Adjust seasonings with salt and pepper. Serve hot or at room temperature.

NOTE

You must reconstitute the chipotles in water before use. In a small bowl pour enough boiling water over the chipotles to cover. Let sit for 30 minutes. Drain and use as directed. Chipotle peppers in adobo sauce can be substituted; chop and use as directed.

NEW ORLEANS RED BEANS AND RICE

For a lower-fat alternative, reduce the vegetable oil to 1 tablespoon, omit the ham hock, and substitute turkey kielbasa for the sausage. You can substitute cranberry or rattlesnake beans for the pintos. Icy cold beer and corn bread muffins would round out this one-bowl supper nicely.

SERVES 8

16 ounces dried pinto or red kidney beans
2 tablespoons vegetable oil
3 onions, halved, peeled and thinly sliced
6 garlic cloves, chopped
2 green bell peppers, seeded and thinly sliced
1 tablespoon ground cumin
½ teaspoon red pepper flakes
Salt and freshly ground black pepper

12 cups beef stock
1 smoked ham hock
2 bay leaves, crumbled
2 pounds sliced andouille or kielbasa sausage
1 (28 ounce) can chopped tomatoes
    with their juice
1 cup uncooked long-grain rice
½ cup chopped fresh parsley
Tabasco

The night before: Spread the beans out on a baking sheet and pick through to remove any small stones or debris. Place the beans in a colander and rinse under cold running water for 1 minute. Transfer the beans to a 5½-quart Dutch oven, add enough water to cover them by 3 inches, and soak the beans overnight. Drain. (Alternately, place the beans in the Dutch oven with enough water to cover, bring them to a full, rolling boil, cover, and turn off the heat. Let the beans soak for 1 hour. Drain the beans in a colander and set aside.)

In a 5½-quart Dutch oven over medium-high heat, heat the oil until very hot. Add the onions, garlic, and green bell pepper and cook for 10 minutes, or until the vegetables soften. Stir in the cumin, red pepper flakes, and salt and pepper to taste. Cook for 1 minute.

Add the drained pinto or kidney beans along with the beef stock, ham hock, and bay leaves. Cover and simmer the beans for 2 hours.

Remove the ham hock. When it is cool enough to handle, remove the meat from the bones. Set the meat aside and discard the bones.

Stir the andouille or kielbasa sausage, tomatoes, and rice into the Dutch oven. Simmer, partially covered, for 25 minutes or until the rice is tender.

Stir in the chopped parsley and reserved ham meat. Season to taste with additional salt and pepper. Spoon into individual bowls and serve at once. Pass the Tabasco separately.

30

BULGUR PILAF

Bulgur wheat is now available in most large grocery stores as well as at health food stores. For this recipe, there is no need to soak the bulgur.

SERVES 8 AS A SIDE DISH

4½ cups chicken stock
3 garlic cloves, chopped
4 green onions, chopped
2 ribs of celery, thinly sliced
3 carrots, shredded
1 cup sliced button mushrooms
¼ cup chopped fresh parsley
Juice of 1 lemon
Salt and freshly ground black pepper
2 cups uncooked bulgur
½ cup chopped fresh basil
1 cup pimento-stuffed green olives, thinly sliced

In a 4½-quart Dutch oven bring the chicken stock to a boil. Add the garlic, green onions, celery, carrots, mushrooms, parsley, lemon juice, and salt and pepper to taste. Return to a boil and cook for 5 minutes. Stir in the bulgur and reduce the heat to a simmer. Cover and cook for 20 minutes, or until the grain is tender and most of the liquid has been absorbed. Remove from the heat and stir in the chopped basil and sliced olives. Cover and let sit for 10 minutes before serving.

SAFFRON-INFUSED COUSCOUS WITH VEGETABLES AND DRIED CRANBERRIES

If you omit the feta cheese in this recipe you have a virtually fat-free dish.

SERVES 8 AS A SIDE DISH, 4 TO 6 AS AN ENTREE

8 cups chicken stock
1 small butternut squash, peeled, cored, and
  cubed into 1-inch pieces
1 (15½ ounce) can chickpeas, rinsed and drained
2 medium carrots, thinly sliced
2 ribs of celery, chopped
4 green onions, chopped
1 (16 ounce) can diced tomatoes with juice
½ teaspoon saffron threads
Juice of 2 lemons

Grated zest of 2 lemons
3 cups couscous
1 teaspoon paprika
½ teaspoon ground coriander
½ teaspoon ground cinnamon
¼ teaspoon cayenne pepper
⅓ cup chopped fresh cilantro
1 cup dried cranberries
Salt and freshly ground black pepper
⅔ cup crumbled feta cheese

In a 5½-quart Dutch oven bring the chicken stock to a boil. Add the butternut squash. Cover and simmer for 20 minutes. Add the chickpeas, carrots, celery, green onions, and tomatoes. Cover and cook for 20 minutes, or until the carrots are tender.

In a small bowl soak the saffron threads with the lemon juice and zest. Let sit for 5 minutes. Add this to the Dutch oven along with the couscous, paprika, coriander, cinnamon, cayenne pepper, cilantro, dried cranberries, and salt and pepper to taste. Cover and let rest off the heat for 5 to 7 minutes, or until all the liquid has been absorbed.

Serve at once, sprinkled with feta cheese.

ROOT VEGETABLE GRATIN

Tender root vegetables bubbling with a thick, creamy cheese sauce makes a meal in itself when paired with a simple green salad and a hearty loaf of multi-grain bread. I use a mandoline to slice the vegetables as thinly as possible. A food processor fitted with the 1-mm slicing disc would work as well. (As a last resort, practice your knife techniques. Just remember to keep those fingers bent under when slicing.)

SERVES 8

10 garlic cloves, thinly sliced

2 pounds russet potatoes, scrubbed, and very thinly sliced (do not peel)

2 pounds sweet potatoes, peeled and very thinly sliced

2 pounds turnips, peeled and thinly sliced

3 onions, thinly sliced

4 carrots, thinly sliced

4 parsnips, peeled and thinly sliced

½ cup cornstarch

4 cups whole milk

2 cups chicken stock

1 cup sour cream

Salt and freshly ground black pepper

3 cups grated Swiss or Gruyère cheese

¾ cup freshly grated Parmesan cheese

1 teaspoon paprika

Preheat the oven to 400°F. Lightly coat the inside of a 5½-quart oval Dutch oven with nonstick cooking spray. Set aside.

In a large bowl toss together the garlic, potatoes, sweet potatoes, turnips, onions, carrots, and parsnips. In a medium bowl whisk together the cornstarch, milk, chicken stock, and sour cream.

Alternately layer the sliced vegetables and the grated Swiss or Gruyère cheese in the Dutch oven, seasoning each vegetable layer generously with salt and pepper. Pour the milk mixture over the vegetables. Cover and bake for 1 hour and 15 minutes. In a small bowl mix together the Parmesan cheese and paprika. Sprinkle this on top of the gratin. Return to the oven and bake, uncovered, for 20 to 30 minutes, or until a golden brown crust has formed on the top. Remove from the oven and let the gratin cool for 10 minutes before serving.

Seafood

FIRECRACKER COCONUT FRIED SHRIMP
WITH WASABI SESAME SAUCE

CURRIED SHRIMP RISOTTO

SPICY SHRIMP AND CHICKEN ETOUFFEE
WITH JASMINE RICE

LOW COUNTRY SHRIMP BOIL

MOROCCAN TUNA STEAKS
WITH STEAMED AROMATIC VEGETABLES

SAVORY SEAFOOD IN SPINACH SAUCE

POACHED SALMON WITH LEMON DILL BUTTER SAUCE

PAN-ROASTED LITTLENECK CLAMS WITH PANCETTA

STEAMED SEAFOOD DUMPLINGS
WITH ASIAN CONDIMENTS

FIRECRACKER COCONUT FRIED SHRIMP WITH WASABI SESAME SAUCE

The spiciness of this delicious shrimp comes from the cayenne pepper and Tabasco in the batter as well as the wasabi in the dipping sauce. The heat is balanced with the flavors of sweet coconut and nutty sesame seeds.

SERVES 4 AS AN ENTREE, 8 TO 10 AS AN APPETIZER

WASABI SESAME SAUCE

⅓ cup wasabi (Japanese horseradish) powder
2 tablespoons lemon juice
½ cup soy sauce
1 tablespoon dark Asian sesame oil
1 tablespoon sesame seeds, lightly toasted

COCONUT SHRIMP

1½ pounds large shrimp, shelled and deveined, tails left on
½ teaspoon cayenne pepper
2 teaspoons dry English mustard, such as Coleman's
1 cup all-purpose flour
1 egg, lightly beaten
1 cup half and half
1 teaspoon Tabasco
1½ cups unsweetened shredded coconut
½ cup bread crumbs
½ cup sesame seeds
About 8 cups peanut oil for deep-frying

Make the Wasabi Sesame Sauce: In a small bowl mix the wasabi powder with enough cold water to make a stiff paste. Cover and set aside for 30 minutes. In a small bowl whisk together the lemon juice, soy sauce, and sesame oil. Add the wasabi paste a little at a time, whisking after each addition and tasting for the amount of heat you prefer. Stir in the sesame seeds and pour the dipping sauce into a small serving bowl.

Prepare the shrimp: With paper towels dry each piece of shrimp. Combine the cayenne pepper, dry mustard, and flour in one bowl, the egg, half and half, and Tabasco in another bowl and the coconut, bread crumbs, and sesame seeds in a third bowl. Dip each shrimp into the flour mixture, then in the egg mixture, and finally, roll the shrimp evenly in the coconut mixture. Place the shrimp on wax paper and chill in the refrigerator for about 30 minutes.

When ready to cook, pour peanut oil into a 5½-quart Dutch oven to a depth of 3 to 4 inches. Heat the oil over medium-high heat until it reaches a temperature of 365°F to 375°F. When the oil has reached the correct temperature, fry the shrimp in batches. (Do not overcrowd the Dutch oven with too many shrimp at once.) Turn the shrimp once during the cooking process and cook until they are golden brown, about 1 to 2 minutes. Remove the shrimp with tongs or a slotted spoon and drain on paper towels. Keep warm until all the shrimp are fried and you are ready to serve. Serve the shrimp with the Wasabi Sesame Sauce.

NOTE

I usually buy my peanut oil for frying in 1-quart bottles. This oil cannot be reused and must be discarded. After frying the shrimp and once the oil has cooled, I funnel it back into the original container, tightly screw on the lid and discard the whole bottle.

CURRIED SHRIMP RISOTTO

This dish utilizes ingredients from the very diverse cuisines of Italy, India, and Thailand.

SERVES 6

8 cups chicken stock or vegetable stock
2 tablespoons olive oil
2 onions, chopped
3 garlic cloves, chopped
1 tablespoon hot or mild curry powder, preferably Madras
3 cups Arborio rice
Grated zest of 1 lime

Juice of 1 lime
1 pound large shrimp, peeled and deveined
⅔ cup coconut milk
¼ cup tightly packed whole basil leaves
1 tablespoon chopped fresh cilantro
Freshly ground black pepper
2 green onions, chopped
⅓ cup chopped toasted peanuts

In a 2½-quart saucepan, bring the stock to a boil. Maintain heat at a simmer and set aside.

In a 4½-quart Dutch oven heat the olive oil over medium-high heat. Add the onions and garlic. Cook until soft but not brown, about 3 to 4 minutes. Add the curry powder and rice. Continue cooking, stirring constantly, until the rice grains are well coated and begin to puff, about 2 minutes. Add the lime zest and juice. Mix well.

Gradually add the simmering stock, ½ cup at a time, stirring frequently and letting the rice completely absorb the stock between additions. Continue stirring, adding the stock ½ cup at a time until all the stock has been used. This whole process should take about 20 minutes.

Add the shrimp and coconut milk. Stir until the coconut milk is nearly absorbed and the shrimp begin to curl. Stir in the basil and cilantro. Remove from the heat, cover, and let sit for 5 minutes.

Transfer to a serving dish and season with pepper to taste. Top with green onions and chopped peanuts. Serve at once.

SPICY SHRIMP AND CHICKEN ETOUFFEE WITH JASMINE RICE

When making an étouffée, it is imperative to brown the roux slowly in order to develop the rich brown color and definitive taste that bind the other flavors in the dish together. Filé gumbo is ground sassafras leaves used as a flavoring and thickener in many Cajun recipes. You can find it in the spice section of most large grocery stores.

Serves 8

⅓ cup vegetable oil
⅓ cup all-purpose flour
3 ribs of celery, chopped
2 onions, chopped
1 green bell pepper, seeded and chopped
6 garlic cloves, chopped
4 cups clam juice or chicken stock
2 tablespoons Worcestershire sauce
1 to 2 teaspoons Tabasco
Salt and freshly ground black pepper

1 bay leaf, crumbled
1 tablespoon fresh thyme leaves
1 tablespoon chopped fresh rosemary
6 boneless, skinless chicken breasts, cut into
   1-inch chunks
1 pound medium shrimp, peeled and deveined
½ cup chopped fresh parsley
1 to 2 tablespoons filé powder
Jasmine Rice (recipe follows)
Tabasco

In a 5½-quart Dutch oven combine the oil and the flour and cook over medium heat, stirring constantly, until the mixture, or roux, is a dark caramel color, about 15 to 20 minutes. Be very careful not to burn the roux or a scorched taste will pervade the dish.

Stir in the celery, onions, green pepper, and garlic and cook for 5 to 7 minutes, stirring occasionally. (At this stage the mixture can be cooled, packed in zip-top freezer bags, and refrigerated or frozen for later use.) Add the clam juice or chicken stock, Worcestershire sauce, Tabasco, salt and pepper to taste, bay leaf, thyme, rosemary, and chicken. Bring the mixture to a boil, reduce the heat to a simmer, and cook, uncovered, for 12 to 15 minutes, or until the chicken is cooked through. Add the shrimp and cook 5 to 7 minutes, or until the shrimp are a bright coral pink and begin to curl. Stir in the parsley and the filé powder. Serve at once over hot Jasmine Rice sprinkled with additional Tabasco if desired.

40

JASMINE RICE

MAKES ABOUT 8 SERVINGS
3½ cups jasmine rice
8 tablespoons (1 stick) butter
Salt and freshly ground black pepper
6 cups chicken stock

Rinse the rice in cold water to remove any impurities. Drain the rice and place it in a 4½-quart Dutch oven.

Add the butter, salt and pepper to taste, and chicken stock. Bring to a boil over high heat. Stir, reduce the heat to low, cover, and simmer the rice for 20 minutes without removing the lid.

Remove the Dutch oven from the heat and let sit for 10 minutes. Remove the lid and fluff the rice gently to separate the grains.

LOW COUNTRY SHRIMP BOIL

A Low Country shrimp boil is to the South what a lobster boil or clambake is to the Northeast. I first had this wonderful Carolina coast seafood supper at the home of my dear friend and mentor, Nathalie Dupree. It is perfect for a large, casual gathering of good friends, who are uninhibited enough to dive into the dish with their bare fingers. Ice-cold beer complements the spiciness of the seafood, vegetables, and broth very nicely.

SERVES 8

2 pounds spicy pork link sausages
2 tablespoons Old Bay Seasoning
1 bunch parsley, tied with kitchen twine
4 quarts water
4 ribs of celery, thinly sliced
12 small new potatoes, scrubbed and halved
24 cloves of garlic (about 2 heads), peeled
4 onions, peeled and quartered
2 banana peppers, thinly sliced

2 lemons, sliced
3 bay leaves
1 cup apple cider vinegar
2 teaspoons salt
1 tablespoon black pepper
8 ears yellow corn, husked, silks removed, and broken in halves
1 to 2 tablespoons Tabasco
4 pounds jumbo shrimp in their shells
Bottled cocktail sauce

In an 8½-quart Dutch oven over medium heat fry the sausage links until browned on all sides, about 8 minutes. Remove the sausage with tongs and drain on paper towels. Discard all but 3 tablespoons of the drippings. Stir in the Old Bay Seasoning, parsley, and water. Bring to a boil and simmer, uncovered, for 10 minutes. Remove the parsley and discard.

Add the celery, potatoes, garlic, and onions. Return to the boil, cover, and cook for 15 minutes. Add the sausage links, banana peppers, lemons, bay leaves, apple cider vinegar, salt, pepper, corn, and Tabasco. Bring to a boil, reduce the heat to medium, cover, and cook for 10 minutes.

Stir in the shrimp and remove the Dutch oven from the heat. Cover and poach the shrimp, off the heat, for 6 to 8 minutes, or until the shrimp have turned a bright coral pink and are just beginning to curl. Do not overcook the shrimp or they will be tough. With a slotted spoon divide the sausage, shrimp, and vegetables among 8 individual bowls. Top each serving with a generous ladle of the broth. Pass the cocktail sauce separately.

42

MOROCCAN TUNA STEAKS WITH STEAMED AROMATIC VEGETABLES

If you prefer, you can substitute salmon, mahi mahi, or sea bass for the tuna.

SERVES 6

1 large onion, chopped
6 garlic cloves, chopped
1 teaspoon turmeric
1 tablespoon ground cumin
1 teaspoon red pepper flakes
½ cup chopped fresh cilantro
¼ cup olive oil
¼ cup lemon juice
6 tuna steaks (about 6 ounces each)

2 onions, thinly sliced
1 (10 ounce) package prewashed spinach,
  stems removed
4 tomatoes, cut into 1-inch cubes
3 carrots, shredded
2 tablespoons chopped ginger
1 cup halved seedless green grapes
Salt and freshly ground black pepper
⅔ cup white wine

In a food processor process the onion, garlic, turmeric, cumin, red pepper flakes, cilantro, olive oil, and lemon juice until mixture is smooth. Rub this paste liberally over the tuna steaks. Cover and refrigerate for 2 hours.

Preheat the oven to 400°F. In a large bowl toss together the onions, spinach, cubed tomatoes, carrots, and ginger. Place in a 5½-quart Dutch oven.

Remove the fish from the refrigerator and place on top of the vegetables. Sprinkle the fish and vegetables with the green grapes and salt and pepper to taste. Pour the wine into the Dutch oven. Cover and bake for about 20 minutes. Remove the cover and continue to bake for 15 minutes.

To check for doneness, gently pull back the flesh of the fish with a fork. It should flake easily. Serve at once, directly from the Dutch oven.

44

SAVORY SEAFOOD IN SPINACH SAUCE

This is an updated version of the classic Seafood Newburg. I have added spinach and egg yolks to enhance the velvety sauce.

SERVES 8

6 cups milk
1 onion, sliced
10 black peppercorns
1 bay leaf
1 parsley stalk
8 tablespoons (1 stick) butter
½ cup flour
4 egg yolks, lightly beaten
⅛ teaspoon ground nutmeg
2 (10 ounce) packages frozen chopped spinach, thawed, drained, and squeezed dry

1 pound large shrimp, peeled, deveined, and coarsely chopped
1 pound bay scallops, rinsed and drained
1 pound lump crab meat, picked over
⅓ cup chopped fresh parsley
2 to 3 tablespoons chopped fresh dill
2 cups freshly grated Parmesan cheese, divided
Salt and freshly ground black pepper
Cooked rice, buttered egg noodles, or baked puff pastry shells

---

Heat the milk in a 3½-quart Dutch oven or saucepan to just below the boil. Add the onion slices, peppercorns, bay leaf, and parsley stalk. Remove from the heat and let the milk sit for 30 minutes. Strain and set aside.

In a 5½-quart Dutch oven melt the butter over low heat. Stir in the flour and cook briefly, about 2 to 3 minutes. Add the infused milk. Cook over low heat for 3 to 4 minutes, or until the white sauce is thick and bubbly.

Place the beaten egg yolks in a small bowl. Add some of the white sauce to the egg yolks to warm them. Add the egg yolk mixture back into the white sauce in the Dutch oven and stir to combine. Stir in the nutmeg and spinach and bring the mixture to a boil, stirring constantly. Add the shrimp, scallops, and crab meat. Reduce the heat to medium and simmer for 3 to 5 minutes, or until the shrimp is cooked through and just beginning to curl.

Remove from the heat and stir in the parsley, dill, and 1½ cups of the Parmesan cheese. Season to taste with salt and pepper.

Ladle the sauce over cooked rice, buttered egg noodles, or baked puff pastry shells. Sprinkle with the remaining Parmesan cheese. Serve at once.

POACHED SALMON
WITH LEMON DILL BUTTER SAUCE

Poaching is an ideal to cook firm fish fillets, as it prevents them from drying out and losing flavor. The poaching liquid should not rise above a simmer or the fish might break apart.

SERVES 6

1 small onion, sliced
4 parsley stalks
1 lemon, sliced
10 black peppercorns
6 (6 ounce) boneless, skinless salmon fillets
Lemon Dill Butter Sauce (recipe follows)

Preheat the oven to 200°F.

In a 5½-quart Dutch oven combine the onion, parsley, lemon, and peppercorns. Add enough water to fill the Dutch oven by half. Bring to a boil, reduce the heat to a simmer, and gently place the salmon fillets into the simmering water. Cover and cook until the salmon flakes easily with a fork, about 10 minutes per inch of thickness. Remove fillets from the stock and drain on paper towels. Wrap in heavy-duty aluminum foil and place in the preheated oven to stay warm.

Place the salmon fillets on individual plates and ladle Lemon Dill Butter Sauce on top. Serve at once.

46

LEMON DILL BUTTER SAUCE

4 egg yolks
Juice of 2 lemons
1 tablespoon chopped lemon zest
2 tablespoons water
8 tablespoons chilled butter, cut into small pieces
Salt and white pepper
2 tablespoons chopped fresh dill
1 tablespoon green peppercorns in brine, rinsed
   and drained

Whisk together the egg yolks, lemon juice, lemon zest, and water in a medium-size heat-resistant glass bowl. In a 2-quart Dutch oven or saucepan set over medium heat bring 2 inches of water to a simmer. Rest the glass bowl on the Dutch oven or saucepan.

Whisk the yolk mixture steadily and do not let it get too hot. It should not exceed 160°F to 180°F or the eggs will scramble. Cook for 5 minutes, whisking constantly, until the mixture is smooth, thick, and lemon yellow.

Slowly add the chilled butter, piece by piece, whisking after each addition. Be sure the butter is fully incorporated before adding another piece. Season to taste with salt and white pepper. Stir in the chopped dill and green peppercorns. The sauce may be made up to 1 hour ahead and kept warm in the bowl over barely simmering water. Press plastic wrap directly onto the sauce to prevent a skin from forming.

PAN-ROASTED LITTLENECK CLAMS WITH PANCETTA

This is a wonderful starter dish or makes a complete meal when paired with a simple salad and crusty bread. It is imperative to clean the clams extremely well; even a single speck of grit will ruin the enjoyment of this quick and easy indulgence.

SERVES 4 TO 6

About 8 to 10 dozen littleneck clams in the shell
½ pound chopped pancetta or bacon
2 onions, thinly sliced
4 garlic cloves, chopped
3 Roma tomatoes, coarsely chopped
2 fennel bulbs, cored and thinly sliced
  (reserve fronds for garnish)

2 carrots, shredded
2 tablespoons capers
2 tablespoons chopped fresh parsley
2 tablespoons chopped fresh basil
1½ cups dry white wine or unsweetened white
  grape juice or chicken stock
Salt and freshly ground black pepper
Crusty French bread

Wash and scrub the clams in several changes of clean water to remove any dirt or grit. With a sharp paring knife remove any beards from the clams. Set aside.

In a 4½-quart Dutch oven cook the pancetta or bacon over medium-high heat until some of the fat is rendered, about 2 minutes. Add the onion and garlic and continue cooking until the onion is soft, about 5 minutes.

Place the cleaned clams in the Dutch oven and scatter the tomatoes, fennel, carrots, capers, parsley, and basil on top. Pour the wine (or juice or stock) over the vegetables. Season well with plenty of salt and pepper to taste.

Bring the contents of the Dutch oven to a boil. Cover and reduce the heat to medium. Steam for 15 to 18 minutes, or until the clams have opened and the vegetables are tender. Discard any unopened clams. (Alternately, preheat the oven to 400°F. Place the lid on the Dutch oven and roast the clams for 30 minutes, or until the clams have opened and the vegetables are tender. Discard any unopened clams.)

Divide the clams among 4 to 6 serving bowls. Pour the vegetables and broth over the clams. Garnish with the reserved fennel fronds. Serve at once, with crusty French bread to soak up the delicious soup base.

STEAMED SEAFOOD DUMPLINGS WITH ASIAN CONDIMENTS

Whenever I serve these at parties, they hardly ever make it out of the kitchen. My friends tend to eat them hot from the steamer before I have time to put them on a platter.

MAKES ABOUT 5 DOZEN

1 pound medium shrimp, peeled, deveined, and finely chopped

½ pound bay scallops, rinsed and drained

½ pound lump crab meat, picked over

½ small head napa cabbage, cored and very coarsely chopped

3 green onions

2 garlic cloves

½-inch piece of ginger

4 tablespoons soy sauce, divided

1 tablespoon rice wine or dry sherry

1 tablespoon cornstarch

1 tablespoon dark Asian sesame oil

Salt and freshly ground black pepper

2 pounds potsticker wrappers (about 2 packages)

2 cups chicken stock

3 tablespoons chopped ginger

4 green onions, cut into 1-inch pieces

In a food processor combine the shrimp, scallops, crab meat, napa cabbage, whole green onions, garlic, ½-inch piece of ginger, 2 tablespoons of the soy sauce, rice wine, cornstarch, dark Asian sesame oil, and salt and pepper to taste. Process until finely chopped. Refrigerate until ready to use.

To assemble the dumplings, place about 1 tablespoon of the filling in the center of each potsticker wrapper. Brush the edges of the dough with a little water. Fold the edges over to meet like a half moon, press together, and seal or crimp with a fork. Slightly flatten the bottom of the dumplings so they will stand upright when steamed and place them on a baking sheet.

In a 5½-quart Dutch oven combine the chicken stock, the remaining 2 tablespoons of soy sauce, chopped ginger, and the chopped green onions. Place a steamer into the Dutch oven. Arrange half of the dumplings on top of the steamer. Bring the chicken stock to a boil, cover, reduce the heat to low, and steam the dumplings until they are plump and cooked through, about 8 minutes. (Do not begin timing the dumplings until the stock has come to a boil.) Remove the dumplings with tongs and wrap in foil to keep warm. (If necessary, place the wrapped dumplings in a preheated 200°F oven.) Repeat the steaming process with the remaining dumplings, adding more stock or water if needed to the bottom of the Dutch oven.

Place the steamed dumplings on a serving platter. Serve warm with an assortment of dipping choices such as chili oil, soy sauce, rice wine vinegar, hot Chinese mustard, and dark Asian sesame oil.

Poultry

ROAST CHICKEN WITH APPLES AND CRANBERRIES

CHICKEN COUNTRY CAPTAIN

COQ AU VIN

PAPRIKA-ROASTED CHICKEN

TURKEY, SAGE DRESSING, AND KALE CASSEROLE

JAMAICAN JERKED CHICKEN WINGS

COLD POACHED CHICKEN BREASTS
WITH TONNATO HERB SAUCE

DEEP-DISH CHICKEN POTPIE

JUICY TURKEY ROULADES
WITH FRESH TANGERINE CRANBERRY RELISH

ITALIAN CHICKEN MOZZARELLA

ROAST CHICKEN WITH APPLES AND CRANBERRIES

A simple roast chicken is actually one of the most elegant entrees you can serve. In this recipe the entire chicken is infused with the wonderful fall flavors of crisp apples and tart cranberries, and the thick and savory sauce is almost like a chutney. For a variation, I sometimes stir a cup of toasted chopped walnuts into the sauce just before serving.

SERVES 4 TO 6

1 (5 pound) roasting chicken
4 tablespoons butter, softened
Salt and freshly ground black pepper
4 Granny Smith apples, peeled, cored, and
 cut into large chunks
2 red onions, thinly sliced
4 garlic cloves, chopped
1 cup cranberries

Juice of 1 lemon
2 tablespoons chopped ginger
1 tablespoon chopped fresh rosemary
1 cup chicken stock
1 cup apple cider
¼ cup balsamic vinegar
¼ cup honey
¼ cup assorted chopped fresh herbs, such as
 parsley, sage, rosemary, and thyme

Preheat the oven to 425°F. Rub the chicken all over with the softened butter and season well outside and inside the cavity with salt and pepper.

In a 7-quart oval Dutch oven stir together the apples, onions, garlic, cranberries, lemon juice, ginger, and rosemary.

Nestle the chicken in the fruit and vegetables. With kitchen twine, tie the legs together. Add the chicken stock. Cover and bake for 1 hour. Remove from the oven, baste the bird with the pan juices, and add the apple cider. Reduce the oven temperature to 375°F and bake, uncovered, for 45 minutes to an hour, or until the internal temperature of the chicken registers 180°F on an instant-read meat thermometer. (Measure in the thickest part of the thigh.)

Remove the chicken from the Dutch oven. Tent the chicken with aluminum foil and allow it to rest on a cutting board. To the Dutch oven add the balsamic vinegar, honey, and fresh herbs. Bring to a boil and boil steadily until the liquid is reduced by half. Skim off any fat, if desired, and season to taste with salt and pepper. Slice the chicken, place on a serving platter, and pass the reduced fruit and sauce separately.

CHICKEN COUNTRY CAPTAIN

The flavors of India pair with those of Southern cuisine in this dish, said to be F.D.R.'s favorite comfort food whenever he was recuperating at the Little White House in Warm Springs, Georgia.

SERVES 4 TO 6

1 (4 pound) chicken, cut into 8 pieces
1 cup all-purpose flour
1 tablespoon paprika
1 teaspoon ground cumin
¼ teaspoon cayenne pepper
¼ teaspoon ground cinnamon
Salt and freshly ground black pepper
3 tablespoons olive oil
3 tablespoons butter
3 onions, chopped
2 green bell peppers, seeded and chopped
4 garlic cloves, chopped

2 tablespoons mild curry powder, preferably Madras
1 cup red wine
1 (28 ounce) can diced tomatoes with their juice
1 (28 ounce) can crushed tomatoes with purée
1 tablespoon poultry seasoning
2 teaspoons sugar
⅔ cup mango chutney, such as Major Grey's
1 cup golden raisins
8 cups cooked Jasmine Rice (see page 43)

GARNISH

½ cup toasted slivered almonds (see page 112)
4 green onions, chopped

Pat the chicken pieces dry with a paper towel. In a shallow bowl or pie plate combine the flour, paprika, cumin, cayenne pepper, cinnamon, and salt and pepper to taste. Coat the chicken pieces with the flour mixture, shaking off the excess.

In a 7-quart Dutch oven over medium-high heat melt the olive oil with the butter. Add the chicken in batches and lightly brown on both sides, about 4 to 5 minutes per side. Remove the chicken and drain on paper towels.

Add the onions, green bell peppers, garlic, and curry powder to the Dutch oven. Cook over medium heat until the onions and peppers begin to wilt, about 5 minutes. Add the red wine and cook until the liquid has almost evaporated, about 10 minutes. Stir in the diced tomatoes, crushed tomatoes, poultry seasoning, and sugar. Bring to a boil, cover, reduce the heat to a simmer, and cook for 30 minutes.

Stir in the chutney, chicken, and raisins. Cover and simmer for 30 to 45 minutes, or until the chicken is tender and cooked through.

Spoon the Jasmine Rice onto a large platter. Arrange the chicken over the rice. Spoon the sauce liberally over the chicken. Sprinkle with the toasted almonds and green onions and serve.

COQ AU VIN

Literally translated "chicken in wine," this is classic French bistro cooking at its best. A simple cheese and fresh fruit course with crusty French bread would be a delightful way to complete this meal.

SERVES 4 TO 6

3 tablespoons olive oil

1 (4 pound) chicken, cut into 8 pieces

½ cup all-purpose flour, lightly seasoned with salt and pepper

⅓ cup brandy

3 cups red wine

2 cups chicken stock

¼ cup balsamic vinegar

1 tablespoon coarse-grained Dijon-style mustard

About 36 red or yellow pearl onions, peeled

1 (16 ounce) can chopped tomatoes with their juice

4 garlic cloves, thinly sliced

1 pound baby carrots, scraped

3 ribs of celery, cut on the diagonal into ¼-inch pieces

3 cups sliced button mushrooms

2 tablespoons chopped fresh rosemary

Salt and freshly ground black pepper

¼ cup chopped fresh parsley

Preheat the oven to 400°F.

In a 5½-quart Dutch oven heat the olive oil over medium-high heat until sizzling. Dredge the chicken pieces in the seasoned flour and then place 3 or 4 pieces in the hot oil, skin side down. Brown the chicken in batches, turning, until lightly browned on all sides. Do not overcrowd the pan with chicken or you will not get a nice browning of the skin. Transfer the chicken to a plate lined with paper towels to drain.

Immediately return the Dutch oven to the heat and add the brandy to deglaze. With a wooden spoon, scrape up any browned bits that have accumulated in the pan. Stir in the red wine, chicken stock, balsamic vinegar, mustard, pearl onions, chopped tomatoes, garlic, carrots, celery, mushrooms, rosemary, and salt and pepper to taste. Bring to a boil, add the chicken to the pan, cover with a tight-fitting lid, and place in the oven.

Bake, gently stirring every 20 minutes or so, for 2 hours, or until the chicken is very tender.

Transfer the chicken pieces to a serving platter. Place the Dutch oven on the stove top and bring to a boil. Reduce the sauce on top of the stove until it is nicely thickened, about 8 to 10 minutes. Ladle the sauce and vegetables over the chicken and top with the chopped parsley. Serve at once.

PAPRIKA-ROASTED CHICKEN

SERVES 4 TO 6

1 (5 pound) chicken
⅓ cup paprika
2 tablespoons ground cumin
½ teaspoon salt
½ teaspoon black pepper
2 tablespoons olive oil
1 head of garlic (about 12 cloves), peeled
2 onions, peeled and quartered
Zest of 3 oranges

2 cups chicken stock, divided
Juice of 3 oranges
¼ cup assorted chopped fresh herbs, such as
  parsley, rosemary, tarragon, and basil
1 pound rutabagas, peeled and cut into large
  chunks
1 pound sweet potatoes, peeled and cut into
  large chunks
1 pound baby carrots, scraped
3 tablespoons chopped fresh parsley

Preheat the oven to 425°F. Lightly pat the chicken dry with paper towels. In a small bowl combine the paprika, cumin, salt, and pepper. Brush the bird with the olive oil, then coat completely and evenly with the spice blend. Carefully stuff the garlic cloves, onion quarters, and orange zest inside the cavity of the bird. Tie the legs together with kitchen twine and place in a 7-quart Dutch oven. Pour 1 cup of the chicken stock around the bird. Cover and bake for 1 hour.

Meanwhile, in a large bowl mix together the orange juice, fresh herbs, rutabagas, sweet potatoes, and baby carrots. Set aside.

After the chicken has cooked for 1 hour, remove it from the oven and baste the bird with the cooking juices. Surround the chicken evenly with the prepared vegetables, add the remaining 1 cup of the stock, cover, and bake for 1 hour longer, or until the internal temperature reaches 180°F on an instant-read meat thermometer when measured in the thickest part of the thigh.

Transfer the chicken to a cutting board and let rest for 10 minutes. Remove the garlic, onions, and orange zest from the chicken cavity and arrange, along with the roasted vegetables, on a large platter. Season to taste with salt and freshly ground black pepper. Place the chicken on top of the vegetables and sprinkle with chopped parsley.

NOTE

If you want, bring the liquid remaining in the Dutch oven to a boil over medium-high heat and cook until reduced by half, about 10 minutes. Adjust seasonings with additional salt and pepper and drizzle the thickened juices over the chicken and vegetables.

TURKEY, SAGE DRESSING, AND KALE CASSEROLE

Who says you can have turkey and dressing only once or twice a year? I'll often buy a precooked turkey breast or rotisserie chicken from my grocery store deli so I can enjoy this dish anytime.

SERVES 8

¾ cup (1½ sticks) butter
10 green onions, chopped
1 red onion, chopped
3 garlic cloves, chopped
3 ribs of celery, chopped
1½ cups chopped pecans
4 cups day-old crumbled corn bread
6 cups herbed stuffing mix (such as
   Pepperidge Farms, not crouton-style)
2 tablespoons poultry seasoning

½ cup chopped fresh parsley
2 tablespoons chopped fresh sage
Salt and a generous grinding of black pepper
Dash of freshly grated nutmeg
2 (10 ounce) packages frozen chopped kale,
   turnip greens, or spinach, defrosted and
   squeezed dry
3 cups cooked shredded turkey or chicken
4 eggs, lightly beaten
8 cups chicken stock

In a 5½-quart Dutch oven over medium-high heat melt the butter and add the green onions, red onion, garlic, celery, and pecans. Cook until the vegetables are soft, about 10 minutes.

Remove from the heat and stir in the crumbled corn bread, stuffing mix, poultry seasoning, parsley, sage, salt and pepper to taste, nutmeg, chopped kale, and the turkey or chicken. Add the beaten eggs and chicken stock. Toss to coat completely. Let the casserole sit for 10 minutes to allow the corn bread to absorb the stock.

Preheat the oven to 400°F.

Cover the Dutch oven and bake the casserole for 1 hour. Remove the lid and continue baking for 30 minutes, or until the casserole is heated through and the top is lightly browned. Let sit for 20 minutes before serving.

JAMAICAN JERKED CHICKEN WINGS

The spicy marinade elevates these chicken wings above the ordinary "Buffalo style" so popular today. Served with ice-cold beer to balance the heat, they make wonderful picnic fare, snacks for weekend football watching, or casual munchies for a Saturday night get-together with friends.

SERVES 10 TO 12 AS AN APPETIZER

¼ cup olive oil
½ cup apple cider vinegar
½ cup orange juice
¼ cup freshly squeezed lime juice
⅓ cup brown sugar
8 green onions, chopped
6 garlic cloves, chopped
3 Scotch bonnet or jalapeño peppers, seeded
   and chopped

2 tablespoons fresh thyme leaves
2 tablespoons chopped fresh sage
1 teaspoon allspice
½ teaspoon ground cinnamon
1 teaspoon salt
1 teaspoon black pepper
½ to 1 teaspoon cayenne pepper
4 pounds chicken wings

The night before: In a large bowl combine all the ingredients except the chicken wings. Whisk until the brown sugar has dissolved.

Cut each chicken wing in two at the elbow joint to create a small "drumette" and wing piece. Remove the wing tip if desired. Place the chicken wings in a large glass baking dish. Pour the marinade over the chicken, cover, and refrigerate overnight.

Preheat the oven to 400°F. Place the chicken wings and their marinade in a 5½-quart Dutch oven. Roast, covered, for 1 hour, stirring and basting occasionally with the marinade juices. Remove the lid and cook for 30 minutes, or until the wings are cooked through. Serve directly from the Dutch oven or place the chicken wings on a large platter and pour the juices over them. Serve warm or at room temperature. These wings will keep for about 3 days in the refrigerator.

60

COLD POACHED CHICKEN BREASTS WITH TONNATO HERB SAUCE

Poach the chicken and make the sauce the night before.

SERVES 8

8 large chicken breast halves with rib meat, with skin on and bone in
6 whole eggs
1 tablespoon white wine vinegar
1 (6½ ounce) can tuna packed in oil (do not drain)
¾ cup mayonnaise
½ cup sour cream
1 (3 ounce) package cream cheese, softened

6 anchovy fillets
2 tablespoons capers, rinsed and drained
Juice of 2 lemons
½ cup chopped fresh basil, divided
Salt and freshly ground black pepper
2 heads Boston lettuce, washed, dried, and separated into leaves
4 plum tomatoes, cut into wedges
4 green onions, chopped
Basil sprigs and lemon slices for garnish

The night before or in the morning: Bring a 5½-quart Dutch oven of lightly salted water to the boil. Add the chicken breasts, whole eggs, and white wine vinegar. Reduce the heat to low and gently poach the chicken, covered, for 18 to 20 minutes. Remove from the heat. With a slotted spoon, remove the eggs. Peel the eggs under cold, running water. Place eggs in an airtight container in the refrigerator.

Allow the chicken to cool in its own broth. When it is cool enough to handle, carefully remove the breasts and discard the skin and bones, leaving the breasts intact. Wrap the breasts in plastic wrap and chill for at least 6 hours, or overnight.

In a food processor combine the undrained tuna, mayonnaise, sour cream, cream cheese, anchovies, capers, lemon juice, and ¼ cup of the basil. Process until smooth. Taste for seasoning and add salt and a generous amount of pepper. Transfer the sauce to an airtight container and chill for 6 hours or overnight.

When ready to serve, line a large platter with Boston lettuce. Cut each chicken breast into ⅓-inch diagonal slices and transfer to the platter.

Stir the remaining ¼ cup basil into the sauce and spoon some of the sauce over each breast. Cut the hard-cooked eggs into wedges. Place the egg and tomato wedges around the platter. Sprinkle the green onions on top. Garnish the platter with basil sprigs and lemon slices. Serve the poached chicken with a crusty French bread, Niçoise olives, and cornichons. Pass the remaining sauce separately.

DEEP-DISH CHICKEN POTPIE

SERVES 6

2 tablespoons olive oil
2 onions, chopped
4 carrots, thinly sliced
2 ribs of celery, thinly sliced
2 cups sliced button mushrooms
1 (10 ounce) package frozen tiny English
 peas, defrosted
2 garlic cloves, chopped
1 tablespoon Worcestershire sauce
2 teaspoons chopped fresh rosemary
1 tablespoon chopped fresh sage

1 teaspoon poultry seasoning
3 cups cooked shredded chicken
8 tablespoons (1 stick) butter
½ cup all-purpose flour
½ teaspoon salt
½ teaspoon black pepper
3 cups milk
2 cups grated Swiss, Gruyère, or cheddar cheese
1 sheet puff pastry
1 egg, beaten with 1 tablespoon water
Additional grated cheese

Preheat the oven to 400°F.

In a 3½-quart Dutch oven set over medium high-heat, heat the oil until sizzling. Add the onions, carrots, celery, mushrooms, peas, and garlic. Sauté until the onions begin to wilt and the carrots begin to soften, about 10 minutes. Remove from the heat and stir in the Worcestershire sauce, rosemary, sage, poultry seasoning, salt and pepper to taste, and shredded chicken. Transfer the contents of the Dutch oven to a large bowl and set aside. With a paper towel, wipe out the Dutch oven.

In the same Dutch oven melt the butter over medium heat. Add the flour and the salt and pepper. Cook over medium heat, stirring constantly, until mixture is smooth and bubbly and just begins to turn a light tan color, about 3 minutes. Add the milk, bring to a boil, and cook for 3 minutes. Remove from the heat and add the cheese in handfuls, stirring until it is melted and smooth. Pour the chicken and vegetable mixture into the cheese sauce and stir to combine. Set aside.

On a lightly floured surface, roll the puff pastry into a round. Using the lid of the Dutch oven as a guide, cut the pastry to fit over the chicken mixture. Carefully place the puff pastry on top of the chicken and vegetables. Make a couple of decorative slits in the top of the pastry to allow steam to escape. Lightly brush the puff pastry with the egg glaze.

Bake for 35 to 45 minutes, or until the pastry is puffed and golden and the sauce is hot and bubbly. Remove to a wire rack and allow to cool for 15 minutes before serving. Pass additional grated cheese separately.

JUICY TURKEY ROULADES
WITH FRESH TANGERINE CRANBERRY RELISH

Between Christmas and New Year's Day I usually host a "drop by" buffet for family and friends. These roulades with sweet and tangy relish make a lasting impression at these gatherings. Roulades may seem a bit intimidating to make, but trust me, they are not at all. Just be sure to securely tie the butter-soaked cheesecloth around the rolled and stuffed turkey. This assures that the roulades will hold their shape during baking.

SERVES 10 TO 12

1 (6 to 7 pound) turkey breast, boned into 2 halves or pieces, skin intact
2 cups cooked wild rice
1 pound uncooked sage pork sausage
3 ribs of celery, finely chopped
1 onion, finely chopped
3 garlic cloves, finely chopped
3 eggs, lightly beaten
3 cups corn bread stuffing mix, such as Pepperidge Farms (not crouton-style)

½ cup chopped fresh parsley
2 tablespoons chopped fresh sage
1 tablespoon poultry seasoning
½ teaspoon salt
1 teaspoon black pepper
2 (12 x 16 inch) rectangles of double thickness cheesecloth, soaked in ½ cup melted butter
2 cups chicken stock
Fresh Tangerine Cranberry Relish (recipe follows)

Preheat the oven to 325°F. Place each turkey breast half, skin side down, on a large piece of plastic wrap. Cover with another piece of plastic wrap and pound meat to a thickness of about ½ inch (about 10 x 14 inches in circumference). Set aside.

In a large bowl combine the cooked wild rice, uncooked sausage, celery, onion, garlic, eggs, corn bread stuffing mix, parsley, sage, poultry seasoning, salt, and pepper. Stir to thoroughly combine.

Spread the stuffing mixture on top of each turkey breast to about ¾ inch from the edges of the meat. Starting with the longer end, roll each turkey breast up as you would a jellyroll, then wrap each roulade tightly in the buttered cheesecloth. Tie the ends of the cheesecloth securely with kitchen twine.

Place the roulades side by side in an 8½-quart oval Dutch oven, seam sides down. Pour the chicken stock over and around the roulades.

Cover and bake for 2 to 2½ hours, or until the juices run clear when pierced with a fork. Baste occasionally with the stock and accumulated juices. Remove from the oven. Place the roulades on a cutting board and allow to cool for 20 minutes before unwrapping the cheesecloth.

Slice meat on the diagonal into 1-inch-thick slices and place them overlapping on a large serving platter. Serve warm or at room temperature with Fresh Tangerine Cranberry Relish.

NOTE
To make this dish ahead, bake the roulades and allow to cool. Wrap them with heavy-duty aluminum foil and refrigerate for up to 2 days. Reheat in a 325°F oven for 45 minutes to 1 hour.

FRESH TANGERINE CRANBERRY RELISH

MAKES ABOUT 4 CUPS

1 medium orange
1 lemon
4 tangerines, peeled and seeded
1 (12 ounce) package cranberries
  (about 3 cups)
1 Granny Smith apple, cored and cut into chunks
1 cup sugar
2 tablespoons crystallized ginger, finely
  chopped
¼ teaspoon ground cloves
1 cup lightly toasted chopped pecans

Cut the orange and lemon into eighths and remove the seeds. Do not peel the fruit. Place in a food processor and process until very fine. Transfer to a large glass bowl.

To the food processor add the tangerines, cranberries, and apple and process until coarsely chopped. Stir this into the bowl with the chopped orange and lemon.

Add the sugar, crystallized ginger, cloves, and toasted pecans. Stir until the sugar dissolves. Cover and place in the refrigerator for at least 2 days before serving to give the flavors a chance to blend. This relish will keep up to 3 weeks in the refrigerator.

ITALIAN CHICKEN MOZZARELLA

I usually prepare the marinade for the chicken the evening before a busy day. When I get home, I transfer the chicken to the Dutch oven and, while it is baking, whip up some rice or buttered egg noodles, a quick salad, and a green vegetable.

SERVES 4

1 (6 ounce) can tomato paste
1 (15½ ounce) can diced tomatoes with
  their juice
¼ cup olive oil
¼ cup red wine vinegar
½ cup red wine or chicken stock
1 tablespoon chopped fresh rosemary
1 tablespoon dried Italian seasoning

1 teaspoon celery seeds
1 teaspoon fennel seeds, slightly crushed
¼ to ½ teaspoon red pepper flakes
1 teaspoon sugar
Salt and freshly ground black pepper
1 (4 pound) chicken, cut into 8 pieces
½ cup freshly grated Parmesan cheese
¾ cup shredded part-skim mozzarella cheese

In a large bowl combine the tomato paste, diced tomatoes, olive oil, red wine vinegar, red wine or chicken stock, rosemary, Italian seasoning, celery seeds, fennel seeds, red pepper flakes, sugar, and salt and pepper to taste. Add the chicken, toss to coat completely, cover, and place in the refrigerator for several hours or overnight.

Preheat the oven to 400°F. Place the chicken and marinade in a 5½-quart Dutch oven. Cover and bake for 1 hour, or until the chicken is cooked through and the juices run clear when pierced with a fork. Remove the lid and sprinkle with the Parmesan and mozzarella cheese. Bake for 10 minutes, or until the cheese is melted. Serve at once.

66

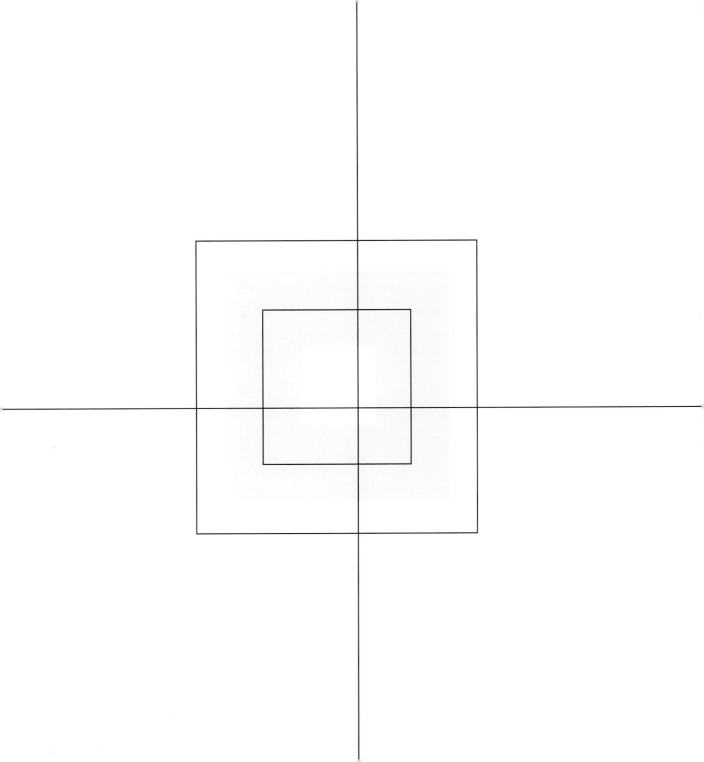

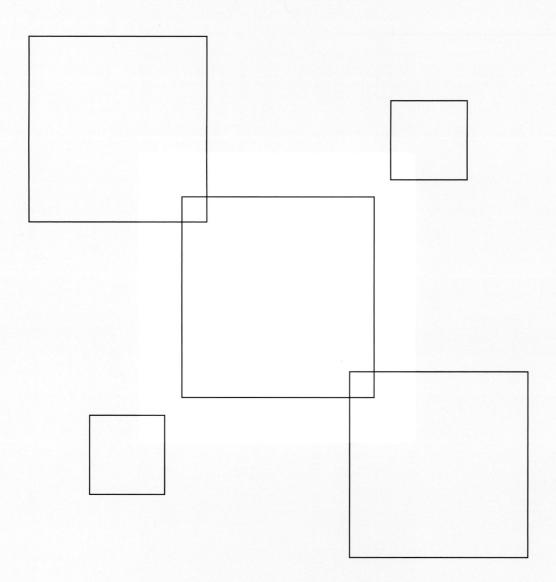

Beef, Veal, and Lamb

CLASSIC BEEF STROGANOFF

BARBECUED BEEF BRISKET

JULIA'S OSSO BUCO MILANESE

VEGETABLE- AND SAUSAGE-STUFFED BRACIOLA

BRAISED BEEF AND VEGETABLES
WITH BRANDY AND MUSTARD SAUCE

BRAISED LAMB SHANKS WITH WHITE BEAN RAGOUT

TRADITIONAL NEW ENGLAND BOILED DINNER

GREEK BRAISED LAMB WITH FENNEL, RUTABAGAS, AND FETA

LAMB MEATBALLS WITH HERBED FETA DIP

CLASSIC BEEF STROGANOFF

This thick and creamy casserole was named in honor of the nineteenth-century Russian diplomat, Count Paul Stroganov. Stroganoff has traditionally been considered a very elegant dish, but these days I find it has a certain comforting charm that makes it perfect for casual dining. In fact, I like to eat it while watching the latest movie rental with the family.

SERVES 8

1 cup red wine or water
1 ounce dried mushrooms
3 pounds very lean boneless sirloin steak, partially frozen and thinly sliced
Salt and freshly ground black pepper
4 tablespoons butter, divided
2 tablespoons olive oil
2 red onions, chopped
2 red bell peppers, seeded and thinly sliced
2 carrots, shredded

4 garlic cloves, chopped
2 cups sliced fresh mushrooms
2 tablespoon all-purpose flour
2 cups beef stock
2 tablespoons Worcestershire sauce
1 tablespoon dry mustard
2 teaspoons dried Italian seasoning
1 (8 ounce) container sour cream
6 cups cooked egg noodles
2 green onions, chopped
2 hard-cooked eggs, peeled and chopped

In a small nonreactive glass bowl combine the red wine and dried mushrooms. Let sit for 1 hour. Lightly season the sliced steak with salt and pepper. In a 5½-quart Dutch oven melt 2 tablespoons of the butter with the olive oil over medium-high heat. Add the steak, red onion, red bell pepper, carrots, garlic, and mushrooms. Cook until the steak is browned and the vegetables are tender, about 15 minutes.

Stir in the reconstituted mushrooms along with their soaking liquid. Cook for 5 to 10 minutes, or until all of the liquid has evaporated. Remove the contents of the Dutch oven to a large bowl and set aside.

Wipe the Dutch oven dry with a paper towel. In the same Dutch oven over medium heat, melt the remaining 2 tablespoons of butter and add the flour, stirring constantly, until the mixture becomes light tan-colored, about 2 minutes.

Add the stock and cook until the mixture reduces by half and is thick and bubbly, about 10 minutes.

In a food processor combine the Worcestershire sauce, dry mustard, Italian seasoning, and sour cream. Process until smooth. Add this to the reduced stock and stir constantly, until it just comes to a boil. Stir in the meat/vegetable mixture and the cooked egg noodles. Cook until just heated through, 4 to 5 minutes. Taste and adjust seasonings with additional salt and pepper. Serve at once, sprinkled with the green onions and chopped egg.

BARBECUED BEEF BRISKET

This brisket can be shredded, then served on buns for sandwiches, or sliced on a diagonal, with the thick barbecue sauce spooned over the slices. Mashed potatoes and hot buttered corn on the cob are great served alongside. This is the perfect make-ahead dish for a beach picnic or symphony in the park.

SERVES 8 TO 10

¼ cup bacon fat or butter, melted
3 onions, thinly sliced
6 garlic cloves, chopped
2 (16 ounce) cans chopped tomatoes with their juice
2 cups tomato purée
¾ cup dark brown sugar
¾ cup balsamic vinegar
1 lemon, thinly sliced

⅓ cup soy sauce
2 tablespoons Worcestershire sauce
Salt and freshly ground black pepper
1 (4 to 5 pound) beef brisket, trimmed of excess fat
½ cup assorted chopped fresh herbs such as parsley, basil, thyme, and rosemary
1 to 2 teaspoons Tabasco (optional)

In a 5½-quart Dutch oven over medium heat combine the bacon fat or butter, onions, and garlic. Cook for about 20 to 25 minutes, or until the onions are a deep mahogany brown. You will need to stir the mixture occasionally to prevent the garlic from burning. Stir in the chopped tomatoes, tomato puree, brown sugar, balsamic vinegar, lemon slices, soy sauce, Worcestershire sauce, and salt and pepper to taste.

Add the brisket and simmer, partially covered, over medium heat for 2 hours. Remove the cover and simmer 45 minutes, or until the sauce is very thick and the brisket is tender. Be sure to stir the sauce every now and then to prevent sticking.

Remove the brisket to a cutting board, leaving the sauce in the Dutch oven. Remove and discard the lemon slices from the sauce. Allow the meat to rest for 15 minutes, then slice or shred as desired.

Stir the fresh herbs and the Tabasco into the sauce. Cook, uncovered, over medium heat for 10 to 15 minutes. Ladle the sauce over the brisket and serve on a platter or in sandwich buns.

JULIA'S OSSO BUCO MILANESE

Osso buco actually means "hollow bone." That's about all that remains on the plate once this comforting Italian "peasant food" supper is finished. I like to serve this with a simple risotto. Gremolata is the garnish of orange zest, garlic, and parsley that traditionally tops the tender shanks. I adapted this recipe from one of Julia Child's. That in itself should tell you how good this dish really is!

SERVES 8

8 veal shanks, about ¾ pound each
Salt and freshly ground black pepper
½ cup all-purpose flour
¼ cup olive oil
3 onions, chopped
4 carrots, coarsely chopped
3 ribs of celery, thinly sliced
7 garlic cloves, chopped

1 cup red wine
1 (28 ounce) can chopped tomatoes with their juice
1 cup beef stock
2 bay leaves, crumbled
¼ cup chopped fresh basil
3 tablespoons tomato paste
Grated zest of 3 oranges
½ cup chopped fresh parsley

Preheat the oven to 400°F. Season the veal shanks with salt and pepper and dredge on both sides in the flour. In a 8½-quart Dutch oven heat the oil over medium heat until sizzling. Add the veal shanks and brown on both sides, about 3 minutes per side. Remove to a plate.

Add the onions, carrots, celery, and half of the chopped garlic to the Dutch oven. Cook for about 10 minutes, until the vegetables begin to caramelize. Stir in the red wine, chopped tomatoes, beef stock, bay leaves, basil, and tomato paste. Nestle the shanks among the vegetables. Bring to a boil, cover, and place in the oven. Cook for about 1½ to 2 hours, or until the shanks are fork-tender. While the shanks are cooking, spoon the sauce over them every 20 minutes or so.

Make the gremolata: In small bowl mix together the orange zest, the remaining half of chopped garlic, and chopped parsley.

Place the veal shanks on a large platter and tent them with aluminum foil to keep them warm. Bring the sauce to a boil, stirring constantly, and cook until the mixture has thickened and reduced by half, about 10 minutes. Taste and adjust seasonings with salt and pepper. Spoon the reduced sauce over the shanks. Sprinkle with the gremolata. Serve at once.

VEGETABLE- AND SAUSAGE-STUFFED BRACIOLA

This recipe was developed by my friend and colleague Virginia Willis, who is now kitchen director for Martha Stewart. It was used in an Italian cooking class she taught at my school in Atlanta. A braciola is a tied, stuffed cut of meat that is slowly braised until it is fork-tender. The meat is then sliced on the diagonal, revealing a stunning spiral of vegetables and sausage inside.

SERVES 6 TO 8

½ cup red wine vinegar
4 tablespoons olive oil, divided
4 garlic cloves, chopped
1 tablespoon black pepper
A 3-pound center-cut top or bottom round steak, about 1 inch thick
1 pound hot Italian sausage, crumbled
2 cups chopped button mushrooms
1 onion, chopped
2 tablespoons chopped fresh basil
1 tablespoon chopped fresh parsley
1 egg, lightly beaten
¼ cup freshly grated Parmesan cheese
Salt and freshly ground black pepper
2 tablespoons butter
1 cup all-purpose flour
2 cups red wine

In a large zip-top freezer bag combine the red wine vinegar, 2 tablespoons of the olive oil, garlic, and pepper. Place the steak in the bag with the marinade and refrigerate for 2 hours or overnight.

In a 5½-quart Dutch oven over medium heat cook the sausage for 5 to 7 minutes, until it is no longer pink. Remove the sausage from the Dutch oven and place in a medium-sized bowl. Leave the drippings in the Dutch oven.

Add the mushrooms and onion to the drippings and cook for 3 to 5 minutes, or until soft. Transfer this to the bowl with the cooked sausage. Add the basil, parsley, egg, and Parmesan cheese to the bowl. Stir well to combine.

Remove the meat from the marinade. Season both sides of the meat with salt and pepper. Place the meat between 2 pieces of plastic wrap and pound with a meat mallet to tenderize and flatten the meat to about ½ inch in thickness.

Place the sausage stuffing on the steak, leaving a 1-inch border around the edges. Starting on the widest side, roll the steak up jellyroll style to form a large cylinder. With kitchen twine, tie the meat

74

in 2-inch intervals along the entire length of the roll.

In the same Dutch oven, cleaned, heat the butter and remaining 2 tablespoons of olive oil over medium-high heat until sizzling. Place the flour in a shallow plate or pie pan. Dredge the meat in the flour to coat and brush off the excess. Place the meat in the hot butter and oil. Brown the roll well on all sides. Add the wine and bring to a boil. (This should happen fairly quickly if your pan is as hot as it should be to get a nice seared crust on the meat.)

Reduce the heat to medium-low and cover. Cook for 1 to 1½ hours, turning occasionally and basting the meat with the wine and juices.

Remove the roll from the Dutch oven and place on a board. Cover the meat with foil and let rest for 15 minutes. Remove the string from the roll and cut the meat into ¾-inch-thick slices. Place the meat on a platter and cover with foil to keep warm.

Bring the wine and meat juices to a boil. Reduce the heat and simmer until slightly thickened. Pour the hot juices over the meat and serve.

BRAISED BEEF AND VEGETABLES WITH BRANDY AND MUSTARD SAUCE

With sun-dried tomatoes, portobello mushrooms, brandy, and red wine, here's a pot roast dinner with a bit of sophistication.

SERVES 6 TO 8

2 tablespoons olive oil
1 (3 to 4 pound) chuck roast, trimmed of all
   visible fat
Salt and freshly ground black pepper
All-purpose flour for dredging
½ cup brandy
½ cup red wine
2 cups beef stock
½ cup balsamic vinegar
¼ cup coarse-grained Dijon-style mustard
10 shallots, peeled

16 to 20 very small red potatoes, scrubbed
16 sun-dried tomatoes, thinly sliced
8 garlic cloves, peeled
1 pound baby carrots, scraped
3 ribs of celery, thinly sliced
2 cups sliced portobello mushrooms
2 tablespoons chopped fresh rosemary
2 tablespoon chopped fresh basil
2 tablespoons chopped fresh parsley
2 bay leaves, crumbled
½ (10 ounce) package prewashed spinach,
   stems removed

Preheat the oven to 325°F. In a 5½-quart Dutch oven over medium-high heat, heat the olive oil until sizzling. Season the chuck roast with salt and pepper and dredge in the flour, shaking off the excess. Brown the chuck roast very well on all sides. Transfer the meat to a plate and set aside.

Immediately return the Dutch oven to the heat and add the brandy and red wine. Cook until the liquid is reduced by half, about 5 minutes. With a wooden spoon, scrape up any browned bits that have accumulated in the pan. Stir in the remaining ingredients except spinach. Bring to a boil, add the meat, cover, and place in the oven. Bake, turning the meat every 30 minutes or so, for 3 hours, or until very tender.

Remove the meat to a cutting board to rest for 10 minutes before slicing. Meanwhile, add the spinach to the sauce remaining in the Dutch oven. Cook, uncovered, over medium-high heat, stirring occasionally, until the sauce is reduced by about a third and the spinach has wilted. Adjust the seasoning with additional salt and pepper. Cut the meat into slices and spoon the sauce and vegetables liberally over the meat.

76

BRAISED LAMB SHANKS WITH WHITE BEAN RAGOUT

White beans enhance the flavor and act as a thickener in this succulent sauce. Slow-braising the lamb will assure that it is fork-tender. And remember that fresh herbs make all the difference in the world.

SERVES 6

6 lamb shanks, about ¾ pound each
Salt and freshly ground black pepper
⅔ cup all-purpose flour
¼ cup olive oil
2 onions, chopped
3 carrots, coarsely chopped
2 ribs of celery, thinly sliced
2 parsnips, peeled and coarsely chopped
3 garlic cloves, chopped
1 cup red wine

1 (16 ounce) can chopped tomatoes with their juice
1 cup chicken stock
2 bay leaves, crumbled
2 tablespoons chopped fresh rosemary
½ cup chopped fresh parsley
3 (15½ ounce) cans white cannellini beans, rinsed and drained, divided
2 tablespoons chopped fresh tarragon
2 tablespoons chopped fresh basil

Preheat the oven to 400°F. Season the lamb shanks with salt and pepper and dredge on both sides in the flour. In a 5½-quart Dutch oven over medium-high heat, heat the oil until sizzling. Add the lamb shanks and brown on both sides, about 5 minutes per side. Remove to a plate.

In the same Dutch oven add the onions, carrots, celery, parsnips, and garlic. Cook over medium heat for about 15 minutes, or until the vegetables begin to soften. Stir in the red wine, chopped tomatoes, chicken stock, bay leaves, rosemary, and parsley.

In a food processor puree one-third of the cannellini beans until smooth. Stir the pureed beans into the vegetable sauce. Nestle the lamb shanks, along with any accumulated juices, among the vegetables. Bring to a boil, cover the Dutch oven, and place in the preheated oven to braise. Cook for about 1½ to 2 hours, or until the meat easily separates from the bone. Spoon the sauce over the shanks every 20 minutes or so.

After the shanks have finished cooking, place them on a large platter and tent them with aluminum foil to keep them warm. Stir the remaining beans and the tarragon into the Dutch oven. Bring the sauce to a boil, stirring constantly, and cook, uncovered, over medium heat for 10 minutes, or until the beans are heated through and the sauce has thickened. Taste and adjust seasonings with additional salt and pepper. Spoon the beans and reduced sauce over and around the shanks. Sprinkle with the chopped basil. Serve at once.

TRADITIONAL NEW ENGLAND BOILED DINNER

Any and all root vegetables work well in this recipe. Use what you have on hand or need to use up quickly.

SERVES 8

1 (4 pound) corned beef brisket
8 new potatoes, scrubbed and halved
8 small boiler onions, peeled
1 pound baby carrots, scraped
4 parsnips, peeled and cut into 2-inch chunks
1 rutabaga, peeled and cut into 2-inch chunks
3 small turnips, peeled and quartered
1 small head green cabbage, cored and cut
    into wedges

1 (16 ounce) can whole beets, rinsed and
    drained
Salt and freshly ground black pepper
¼ cup chopped fresh parsley

HORSERADISH SAUCE

1½ cups sour cream
4 to 6 tablespoons prepared horseradish
2 tablespoons Dijon-style mustard
3 tablespoons apple cider vinegar

Rinse the corned beef under running water and place in an 8½-quart Dutch oven. Cover with cold water and bring to a boil, skimming off any scum that rises to the surface. Reduce the heat to low and simmer, covered, for 3½ hours. (At this point the meat can sit in the hot cooking liquid for up to 2 hours if you wish to delay serving time.) Remove the meat to a carving board and cover loosely with aluminum foil.

To the Dutch oven add the new potatoes, onions, carrots, parsnips, rutabaga, and turnips. Simmer, uncovered, for 30 to 40 minutes, or until the vegetables are quite tender.

Add the cabbage wedges and the beets and cook for an additional 10 minutes. Slice the meat on the diagonal across the grain and place in the center of a large platter. Remove the vegetable from the broth and place them around the meat. Season to taste with salt and pepper. Sprinkle with the chopped parsley just before serving. Serve with the Horseradish Sauce and slices of dark bread.

To make the Horseradish Sauce: In a medium bowl combine all the ingredients. This sauce will keep for 1 week in the refrigerator.

GREEK BRAISED LAMB WITH FENNEL, RUTABAGAS, AND FETA

I love the earthiness and depth of flavor that the fennel and rutabagas add to this Greek-inspired dish.

SERVES 6 TO 8

2 pounds fresh fennel bulbs, cored and cut lengthwise into ¼-inch slices (reserve fennel fronds for garnish)

2 pounds rutabagas, peeled and cut into ¼-inch slices

2 tablespoons olive oil

1 red onion, thinly sliced

3 pounds ground lamb

4 garlic cloves, chopped

2 teaspoons ground coriander seeds

Salt and freshly ground black pepper

¼ cup balsamic vinegar

½ cup coarsely chopped Greek black olives, such as kalamata

⅓ cup chopped fresh cilantro

⅓ cup chopped fresh parsley

4 cups Homemade Vegetable Tomato Sauce (recipe follows) or prepared spaghetti sauce

2 cups freshly grated Parmesan cheese, divided

¾ cup crumbled feta cheese

In a 5½-quart Dutch oven of boiling salted water cook the fennel and rutabaga slices until almost tender, about 15 minutes. Drain and set aside.

Preheat the oven to 350°F. In the same Dutch oven heat the oil over medium heat. Add the red onion, ground lamb, garlic, coriander, and salt and pepper to taste. Cook, stirring constantly, until the lamb is broken up and browned, about 5 to 7 minutes. Remove from the heat and drain any excess fat. Transfer the contents of the Dutch oven to a bowl and stir in the balsamic vinegar, black olives, cilantro, and parsley.

Spoon half of the fennel and rutabaga back into the Dutch oven. Arrange half of the lamb over the vegetables and top with half of the Homemade Vegetable Tomato Sauce. Sprinkle with half of the Parmesan cheese. Repeat this layering with the remainder of the vegetables, lamb, sauce, and Parmesan.

Cover the Dutch oven and bake until the fennel is very tender, about 45 minutes.

Remove from the oven. Top with the feta cheese. Cover and allow the casserole to sit for 15 minutes before serving. Garnish with the reserved fennel fronds.

80

HOMEMADE VEGETABLE TOMATO SAUCE

MAKES ABOUT 4 CUPS

2 tablespoons butter
1 onion, chopped
1 carrot, chopped
2 tablespoons all-purpose flour
1½ cups chicken stock
1 cup red wine
1 (28 ounce) can crushed tomatoes with purée
2 garlic cloves, chopped

1 tablespoon fresh thyme leaves
1 tablespoon chopped fresh rosemary
2 teaspoons sugar
Salt and freshly ground black pepper

In a 3½-quart Dutch oven melt the butter over medium heat, add the onion and carrot and cook until lightly browned, about 15 minutes. Stir in the flour and cook for 2 minutes more. Add the remaining ingredients. Simmer, uncovered, stirring occasionally to prevent sticking, for 1 hour, or until the sauce is dark and thick. This sauce freezes well for 3 months.

LAMB MEATBALLS WITH HERBED FETA DIP

MAKES ABOUT **4 DOZEN**

2 pounds very lean ground lamb
1 onion, finely chopped
2 garlic cloves, finely chopped
3 green onions, finely chopped
2 egg whites, lightly beaten
2 tablespoons chopped fresh mint
1 tablespoon chopped fresh rosemary
2 tablespoons chopped ginger
¼ cup currants
2 teaspoons ground cumin
½ teaspoon cayenne pepper
¼ teaspoon ground cinnamon
Salt and freshly ground black pepper
½ to 1 cup seasoned bread crumbs
¼ cup olive oil
1 (16 ounce) can diced tomatoes with their juice
Juice of 2 lemons
2 tablespoons chopped fresh parsley
2 tablespoons chopped fresh mint
Herbed Feta Dip (recipe follows)

In a large bowl combine the lamb, onion, garlic, green onions, egg whites, mint, rosemary, ginger, currants, cumin, cayenne pepper, cinnamon, and salt and pepper to taste. Add just enough bread crumbs to hold the meatballs together. Shape the mixture into about 60 (1¼-inch) meatballs, place on a baking sheet that has been lined with parchment paper, cover, and refrigerate for 1 hour.

Preheat the oven to 400°F. In a 5½-quart Dutch oven heat the olive oil over medium-high heat. Sauté the meatballs in batches, browning well on all sides. Remove with a slotted spoon to a plate lined with paper towels to drain. When all the meatballs have been browned, discard the oil in the Dutch oven. Return the meatballs to the Dutch oven and top with the diced tomatoes, lemon juice, parsley, and mint. Stir gently to coat the meatballs. Cover and bake for 40 to 45 minutes, or until the meatballs are cooked through and the sauce is bubbly.

Place the meatballs and sauce on a large serving platter. Serve warm with fresh pita bread and the Herbed Feta Dip on the side.

VARIATION
This mixture can also be shaped into a meatloaf and placed in a 3½-quart oval Dutch oven. Top with the sauce, cover, and bake at 400°F for 40 minutes. Remove the cover and continue baking for 25 minutes. Allow the meatloaf to rest for 10 minutes before slicing and serving. Top each serving with the Herbed Feta Dip.

HERBED FETA DIP

MAKES ABOUT 3¹/₂ CUPS

1 cup cottage cheese, drained
½ cup sour cream
1 (8 ounce) package cream cheese, softened
3 green onions, chopped
3 garlic cloves, chopped
1 cucumber, halved and seeded, coarsely
   chopped and patted dry with paper towels
   (do not peel)

3 tablespoons chopped fresh dill
1 tablespoon Worcestershire sauce
1 cup crumbled feta cheese
Salt and freshly ground black pepper

In a food processor combine the cottage cheese, sour cream, cream cheese, green onions, and garlic. Process until fairly smooth. Remove to a medium bowl and stir in the cucumber, dill, Worcestershire sauce, feta cheese, and salt and pepper to taste. Cover and chill. This dip will keep about 5 to 7 days in the refrigerator.

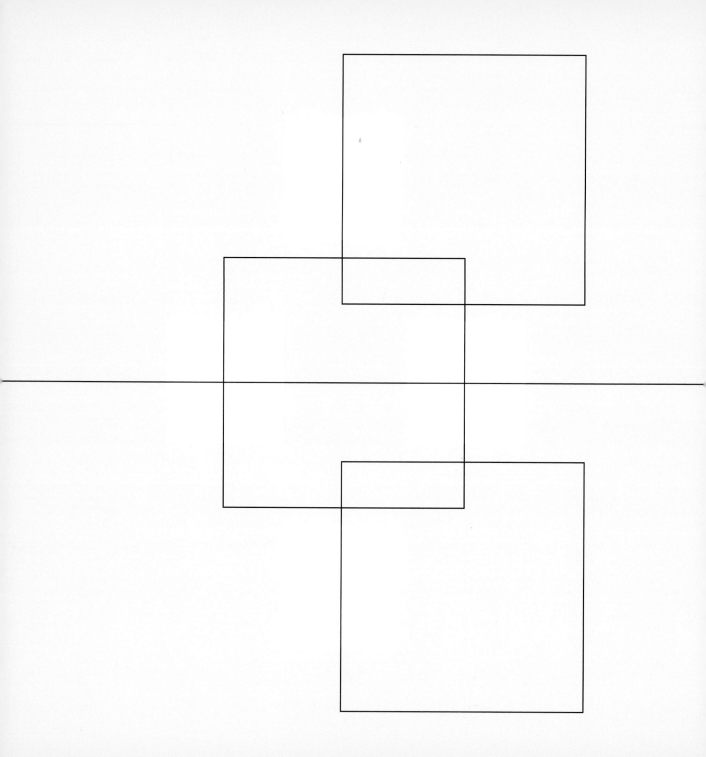

Pork

PARMESAN CHEDDAR GRITS PUDDING
WITH COUNTRY HAM

WINE-BRAISED CHORIZO SAUSAGES
WITH HONEY MUSTARD SAUCE

ASIAN-STYLE BRAISED PORK RIBS

OKTOBERFEST BRATWURST WITH CARAWAY NOODLES

MOLASSES-GLAZED PORK WITH DRIED FRUIT

ASIAN HOT AND SOUR MEATBALLS

CHINESE-STYLE BRAISED PORK LOIN

BRAISED PORK LOIN IN MILK

SAVORY CHOPPED PORK
WITH TWELVE OAKS BARBECUE SAUCE

QUICK AND CONVENIENT CASSOULET

PARMESAN CHEDDAR GRITS PUDDING WITH COUNTRY HAM

Sunday brunch is my preferred time to entertain, and this is one of my favorite casseroles to serve. It can be assembled entirely the night before, covered and refrigerated, then baked just before your guests arrive.

SERVES 8

8 tablespoons (1 stick) butter
6 cups milk
1 cup heavy cream
2½ cups long-cooking regular grits
2 (10 ounce) packages frozen chopped
  spinach, defrosted and squeezed dry

8 green onions, chopped
3 garlic cloves, chopped
2 cups shredded cheddar cheese
3 eggs, lightly beaten with ½ cup sour cream
Salt and freshly ground black pepper
2 cups cooked, coarsely chopped country ham
1 cup freshly grated Parmesan cheese

Preheat the oven to 375°F.

Combine the butter, milk, and cream in a 3½-quart Dutch oven and heat nearly to the boil. Stir in the grits and cook for 20 to 25 minutes, stirring as necessary to prevent sticking. Remove from the heat and stir in the spinach, green onions, garlic, and cheddar cheese.

Stir in the eggs whisked with the sour cream. Season to taste with salt and pepper. Fold in the chopped ham.

Cover and bake for 30 minutes. Sprinkle with the Parmesan cheese and bake, uncovered, for 15 minutes, or until the top is golden. Remove from the oven and let the casserole rest for 10 minutes before serving.

WINE-BRAISED CHORIZO SAUSAGES WITH HONEY MUSTARD SAUCE

Chorizo is a very spicy Spanish sausage. You can substitute andouille or, for a milder taste, Polish kielbasa. Let your guest serve themselves with toothpicks or small cocktail forks, or thread 3 to 4 pieces of sausage on wooden skewers.

SERVES 12 AS AN APPETIZER

2 tablespoons olive oil
2 red onions, thinly sliced
1 red bell pepper, seeded and thinly sliced
2 rosemary sprigs
⅓ cup honey
1 tablespoon yellow mustard seeds
3 pounds chorizo, andouille, or kielbasa
   sausage, cut into ¾-inch slices
3 cups dry red wine
Rosemary sprigs for garnish

HONEY MUSTARD SAUCE

½ cup honey
½ cup coarse-grained Dijon-style mustard
1 tablespoon chopped fresh rosemary

In a 5½-quart Dutch oven over medium-high heat, heat the oil until hot. Add the onions, red bell pepper, and 2 rosemary sprigs. Lower the heat to medium and cook until the onions are nearly translucent, about 5 minutes. Stir in the honey, mustard seeds, and sausage. Pour the red wine over the sausage and bring to a boil. Reduce the heat to a simmer and cook, uncovered, until the liquid is absorbed and glazes the sausage. This will take about 30 to 45 minutes. Stir frequently to prevent the sausage from sticking.

Meanwhile, make the Honey Mustard Sauce: In a small bowl mix together all the ingredients. Set aside.

Remove the rosemary sprigs from the Dutch oven and transfer the sausage slices to a serving platter. Garnish with fresh rosemary sprigs. Serve with Honey Mustard Sauce.

VARIATION

For a sweeter glaze, substitute Coca-Cola Classic (not Diet) for the red wine.

ASIAN-STYLE BRAISED PORK RIBS

I love the taste of these unique Asian-style ribs, slightly sweet with just a hint of orange and anise. Slow braising yields a meltingly tender result. These ribs would be perfect as pick-up hors d'oeuvres for a party, or as a main meal served with hot buttered noodles and a crisp green salad.

SERVES 8 TO 10 AS AN APPETIZER, 4 TO 6 AS AN ENTREE

4 pounds country-style pork ribs, cut into 2-inch pieces
½ cup hoisin sauce
1½ cups chicken stock
½ cup dry sherry or rice wine
3 tablespoons soy sauce
2 tablespoons dark Asian sesame oil
⅔ cup chili sauce (such as Heinz) or tomato sauce
3 tablespoons chopped ginger

4 garlic cloves, sliced
6 green onions, cut into 1-inch pieces
Zest of 2 oranges
3 tablespoons brown sugar
1 or 2 whole star anise

GARNISH

2 green onions, cut in half and thinly sliced lengthwise
Zest of 1 orange
Sesame seeds

Trim and discard the extra fat from the ribs. Place the ribs in a 5½-quart Dutch oven, cover with water, and bring to a boil. Cook for 15 minutes. Drain and return the ribs to the Dutch oven.

In a large bowl combine the remaining ingredients. Pour the sauce over the ribs, bring to a boil, cover, and reduce the heat to a simmer. Cook, stirring occasionally, until the ribs are very tender and the meat separates easily from the bone, about 1½ to 2 hours. Be careful not to allow the ribs to stick or they will develop a scorched taste. (Alternately, preheat the oven to 400˚F. Pour the sauce over the ribs, cover the Dutch oven, and bake for 1½ to 2 hours, or until the ribs are very tender and separate easily from the bone.)

Remove the lid during the last 15 minutes of cooking time so the sauce reduces and thickens slightly. Serve on a large platter, spooning the thickened sauce over the ribs. Garnish with the slivered green onions, additional orange zest, and sesame seeds.

OKTOBERFEST BRATWURST WITH CARAWAY NOODLES

This is an October tradition at my house, and my long-time friends know when I serve this dish that it signals the beginning of shorter days and crisp autumn weather. I accompany this with dark bread and mustards, and serve it with an assortment of beers, fresh fruit, and a sampling of rich imported cheeses.

SERVES 8

3 tablespoons vegetable oil
3 Granny Smith apples, peeled, cored, and sliced
3 onions, sliced
2 cups thinly sliced button mushrooms
16 large, fresh German bratwurst sausages, pricked all over with a fork
1 (12 ounce) bottle dark beer
1 (12 ounce) package egg noodles, cooked according to package directions, drained
1 (15½ ounce) can sauerkraut, rinsed and drained

2 (15½ ounce) cans white beans, rinsed and drained
2 tablespoons coarse-grained Dijon-style mustard
1½ cups shredded Swiss cheese
1½ tablespoons caraway seeds, slightly crushed
Salt and freshly ground black pepper
¼ cup chopped fresh parsley

ACCOMPANIMENTS
Pumpernickel bread
Assorted mustards

Heat the vegetable oil in a 5½-quart Dutch oven over medium-high heat. Add the apples, onions, and mushrooms. Cook until the onions are soft and the mushrooms brown slightly, about 8 to 10 minutes. Remove to a bowl and set aside.

Add the sausages to the hot Dutch oven in 2 batches and brown them well on all sides, using tongs to turn them, about 7 minutes per side. Transfer the sausages to a plate lined with paper towels to drain.

Add the beer to the Dutch oven and boil for 1 minute, scraping any sausage bits from the bottom of the Dutch oven. Reduce the heat to medium and add the sausages back in. Cover and cook for 15 to 20 minutes, or until the sausages are cooked through. Remove the sausages from the Dutch oven.

Preheat the oven to 400°F. To the Dutch oven add the reserved apples, onions, and mushrooms, along with the cooked egg noodles, sauerkraut, white beans, Dijon mustard, Swiss cheese, caraway seeds, and salt and pepper to taste. Nestle the sausages on top of the noodles. Cover and bake for 20 minutes, or until the mixture is heated through and the cheese has melted.

Sprinkle with chopped parsley. Serve warm, with pumpernickel bread and assorted mustards on the side.

MOLASSES-GLAZED PORK WITH DRIED FRUIT

For this elegant entree you will need to soak the fruit the night before. I keep dried fruit on my pantry shelf year-round, but it is especially welcome in the winter months. This is delicious the next day, sandwiched inside piping hot biscuits.

SERVES 8

2 pounds mixed dried fruit such as figs, apricots, apples, peaches, prunes, dark and golden raisins, cherries, and cranberries
½ cup dry sherry
¼ cup balsamic vinegar
1 cup orange juice
8 tablespoons (1 stick) butter
2 red onions, thinly sliced
1 tablespoon mild curry powder, preferably Madras
2 tablespoons chopped fresh rosemary
¾ cup molasses
1 teaspoon paprika
½ teaspoon ground cinnamon
¼ teaspoon allspice
Dash of freshly grated nutmeg
2 cups apple juice or cider
1 (4 pound) boneless pork loin
Salt and freshly ground black pepper

The night before: In a large glass bowl combine the fruit with the sherry, balsamic vinegar, and orange juice. Cover and allow the fruit to soak overnight (at least 8 hours).

Preheat the oven to 325°F. In a 5½-quart Dutch oven melt the butter over medium heat. Add the onions, curry powder, and rosemary and cook until the onions are soft, about 5 minutes. Stir in the molasses, paprika, cinnamon, allspice, and nutmeg. Add the soaked fruit, with any remaining liquid, and apple juice or cider. Stir until well combined.

Season the pork loin with salt and pepper. Place in the Dutch oven and spoon some of the fruit and sauce over the pork. Cover and roast for 2 hours, basting with the sauce every 20 minutes or so. Remove the lid and roast an additional 30 minutes to brown the pork.

Remove the pork to a cutting board and allow to rest for 10 minutes. Place the Dutch oven on the stove and simmer the fruit and sauce over medium heat until it has thickened. Transfer the fruit to a serving bowl. Slice the pork and place on a serving platter. Pass the dried fruit and sauce separately.

ASIAN HOT AND SOUR MEATBALLS

When browning the meatballs, do not cook them through or they will become dry. They will continue cooking as they simmer in the sauce. This is excellent party fare.

MAKES ABOUT 4 DOZEN

MEATBALLS
1 pound ground pork
1 pound ground turkey
6 green onions, finely chopped
3 garlic cloves, finely chopped
1 small can water chestnuts, rinsed, drained,
   and finely chopped
2 eggs, lightly beaten
2 tablespoons soy sauce
1 tablespoon dark Asian sesame oil
2 tablespoons hot Chinese mustard
3 tablespoons sesame seeds
1 tablespoon ground coriander
1 teaspoon red pepper flakes
¼ teaspoon Chinese 5-spice powder
½ to 1 cup cracker crumbs
¼ cup peanut oil

SAUCE
1 cup brown sugar
1 cup rice wine vinegar
¼ cup soy sauce
2 tablespoons dark Asian sesame oil
1 cup hoisin sauce
1 cup chicken stock
3 tablespoons chopped ginger
¼ cup cornstarch whisked with ½ cup water
1 (16 ounce) can pineapple chunks with juice

TO SERVE
Romaine lettuce leaves
Chopped green onions
Sesame seeds
Soy sauce
Hot Chinese mustard

In a large bowl mix together the ground pork, ground turkey, green onions, garlic, water chestnuts, eggs, soy sauce, sesame oil, hot mustard, sesame seeds, ground coriander, red pepper flakes, and Chinese 5-spice powder. Stir in enough cracker crumbs to give the meat a stiff consistency.

Shape into 1-inch balls, using about 2 tablespoons of the mixture for each ball. Place the balls on a parchment-lined baking sheet and chill for 30 minutes to 1 hour.

Heat the peanut oil in a 5½-quart Dutch oven over medium-high-heat. Sauté the meatballs in batches until browned all over, being careful not to overcrowd the Dutch oven. Drain on paper

92

towels. Discard the oil in the Dutch oven and return to the stove.

In the same Dutch oven combine the brown sugar, rice wine vinegar, soy sauce, sesame oil, hoisin sauce, chicken stock, and ginger. Bring to a boil, then stir in the cornstarch mixed with the water. As soon as the sauce thickens, stir in the pineapple chunks with their juice. Add the meatballs, cover, and lower the heat to low. Simmer, covered, for 40 to 45 minutes.

When ready to serve, line a large platter with Romaine lettuce leaves and arrange the meatballs and pineapple chunks on top. Sprinkle with additional green onions and sesame seeds. Serve with soy sauce and hot Chinese mustard on the side.

CHINESE-STYLE BRAISED PORK LOIN

For even more flavor, marinate the pork overnight in the refrigerator before cooking. Allow the pork to come to room temperature before slow-braising in the oven.

SERVES 6 TO 8

1 (4 pound) boneless pork loin
Freshly ground black pepper
1½ cups orange juice
⅓ cup dry sherry or Chinese rice wine
½ cup soy sauce
1 cup hoisin sauce
½ cup peanut butter
⅓ cup honey
3 tablespoons uncooked long-grain rice
8 ¼-inch-thick slices of ginger, cut into strips

2 tablespoons chili garlic paste
2 tablespoons fish sauce
2 tablespoons dark Asian sesame oil
6 garlic cloves, thinly sliced
6 green onions, chopped
1 (16 ounce) can crushed pineapple with juice

Preheat the oven to 325°F. Pat the pork loin dry with paper towels and season all over with freshly ground black pepper.

In a large bowl whisk together the remaining ingredients.

Place the meat in a 5½-quart Dutch oven and pour the sauce over the meat. Cover and place in the oven. Cook, basting the pork occasionally, until it is very tender and registers about 160°F on an instant-read meat thermometer, about 2½ to 3 hours. During the last 15 to 20 minutes of cooking time, remove the lid so the sauce reduces and thickens slightly.

Remove from the oven and place the pork on a cutting board. Allow the pork to rest 10 minutes before slicing. Pour the sauce over and around the meat.

BRAISED PORK LOIN IN MILK

I adapted this recipe from one prepared by Antonio Allegranzi, a wonderful Italian chef who has shared his culinary knowledge and master techniques at my school many times. This is now my favorite way to serve pork or veal. Once you have browned the onions you are basically free (except for the occasional stir) to go about other household chores.

SERVES 6 TO 8

1 (4 pound) boneless pork loin or veal roast
Salt and freshly ground black pepper
¼ cup olive oil
4 onions, thinly sliced
6 garlic cloves, chopped
2 tablespoons chopped fresh rosemary
6 cups whole milk
Sprigs of rosemary

Preheat the oven to 325°F. Pat the meat dry with paper towels and season all over with salt and pepper.

In a 5½-quart Dutch oven heat the olive oil over medium-high heat until sizzling. Add the onions and garlic and cook for 20 minutes, or until the onions begin to caramelize. Stir in the chopped rosemary and cook for 1 minute.

Place the pork or veal roast on top of the onions and pour the milk over the meat. Cover and place in the preheated oven. Cook, stirring occasionally, until the meat is very tender and registers about 160°F on an instant-read meat thermometer, about 2½ to 3 hours. During the last 15 to 20 minutes of cooking time, remove the lid so the sauce reduces and thickens slightly.

Remove from the oven and place the meat on a cutting board. Allow the meat to rest 10 minutes before slicing. Arrange the meat slices on a platter. If desired, bring the sauce to a boil and reduce further. Taste and adjust seasonings with additional salt and pepper. Pour the sauce over and around the sliced meat and garnish with fresh sprigs of rosemary.

SAVORY CHOPPED PORK
WITH TWELVE OAKS BARBECUE SAUCE

Bourbon and fresh mint, staples in the Southern Mint Julep, find new life in this spicy-sweet barbecue sauce named after the famed plantation in *Gone with the Wind* where Scarlett first encounters Rhett Butler.

SERVES 8 TO 10

1 (4 to 5 pound) bone-in pork butt roast
2 to 3 teaspoons crushed red pepper flakes
1 tablespoon salt
1 tablespoon black pepper
1 cup apple cider
1 cup apple cider vinegar
4 onions, thinly sliced

4 garlic cloves, chopped
1 green bell pepper, seeded and finely chopped
Twelve Oaks Barbecue Sauce (recipe follows)

The night before: Rub the outside of the pork butt with the red pepper flakes, salt, and black pepper. Place in a zip-top freezer bag and refrigerate overnight.

Remove the pork from the refrigerator and let it sit at room temperature for 1 hour. Preheat the oven to 300°F.

Place the pork butt in a 5½-quart Dutch oven. Pour the apple cider and cider vinegar over and around the pork. Scatter the onions, garlic, and green bell pepper over and around the pork. Cover and roast in the oven for 3½ to 4 hours, or until an instant-read meat thermometer inserted into the pork registers 180°F. Spoon the juices over the pork every 30 minutes during the roasting time. Remove the pork from the pan and let sit for 1 hour before chopping or shredding. Reserve the roasted vegetables and 1 cup of the pan juices.

Chop the pork with a sharp knife or shred the meat by pulling two forks over it. Discard the bone. Combine the chopped pork with the 1 cup of reserved pan juices and all of the vegetables. Ladle the Twelve Oaks Barbecue Sauce over the pork. (Alternatively, the pork can be thinly sliced and topped with the vegetables and sauce.) Pass remaining sauce separately.

TWELVE OAKS BARBECUE SAUCE

¼ cup bacon fat or butter, melted

3 onions, thinly sliced

6 garlic cloves, chopped

1 (16 ounce) can chopped tomatoes with juice

2 cups tomato purée

½ cup Maker's Mark or any other Kentucky bourbon

¾ cup molasses

½ cup apple cider vinegar

Juice of 3 lemons

¼ cup soy sauce

2 tablespoons Worcestershire sauce

Salt and freshly ground black pepper

½ cup assorted chopped fresh herbs, such as parsley, rosemary, and mint

1 teaspoon Tabasco, or to taste

In a 3½-quart Dutch oven set over medium heat combine the bacon fat or butter, onions, and garlic. Cook for about 20 minutes, or until the onions are a deep, dark brown. Stir the mixture occasionally to prevent the garlic from burning.

Stir in the chopped tomatoes, tomato puree, bourbon, molasses, cider vinegar, lemon juice, soy sauce, Worcestershire sauce, and salt and pepper to taste. Simmer, uncovered, over low heat for 1 hour, or until the sauce is very thick. Stir in the fresh herbs and Tabasco and cook for 15 minutes more. Cool. (For a smoother sauce, process the cooled sauce in a food processor until smooth.) Sauce will keep in the refrigerator for up to 1 month.

QUICK AND CONVENIENT CASSOULET

"Quick and convenient" and "cassoulet" sound like a contradiction in terms. Traditionally, a cassoulet can take up to three days to prepare, which can daunt even the most ambitious cooks. I've reduced that time to a few hours without any loss in flavor. This makes a wonderful fireside supper for a crowd, complemented with only a glass of Merlot and crusty French bread.

SERVES 8 TO 10

VEGETABLE SAUCE

½ pound thick-sliced bacon, cut into
   small pieces
4 onions, chopped
6 garlic cloves, chopped
2 (28 ounce) cans chopped plum tomatoes
   with their juice
½ cup balsamic vinegar
2 cups red wine
4 cups beef stock, plus more if needed

MEAT AND SPICES

4 (1-inch-thick) pork loin chops, bone
   and fat removed, cut into cubes
4 (1-inch-thick) lamb loin chops, bone
   and fat removed, cut into cubes
2 whole boned duck or chicken breasts, skin
   on, cut into cubes

2 pounds Polish kielbasa or garlic sausage, sliced
1 teaspoon ground allspice
1 teaspoon poultry seasoning
2 tablespoons brown sugar
Salt and freshly ground black pepper

BEANS AND HERBS

4 (15½ ounce) cans white cannellini beans,
   rinsed and drained
3 bay leaves, crumbled
½ cup chopped fresh parsley
2 tablespoons chopped fresh basil
2 tablespoons chopped fresh oregano

CRUMB TOPPING

3 cups herb-seasoned stuffing mix, such as
   Pepperidge Farms (not crouton-style)
2 tablespoons fresh thyme leaves
8 tablespoons (1 stick) melted butter

In an 8½-quart Dutch oven over medium heat, fry the bacon until crispy brown. Remove and drain on paper towels. Set aside.

In the reserved drippings, sauté the onions and garlic until soft, about 6 to 8 minutes. Add the tomatoes with their juice, balsamic vinegar, red wine, and beef stock. Bring to a boil, reduce the heat to a simmer, cover, and cook for about 30 minutes.

Meanwhile, preheat the oven to 425°F. Line a 15 x 10 x 1- inch jelly roll pan with aluminum foil. In a large bowl toss together the cubed pork, lamb, duck or chicken, and the sausage with the allspice, poultry seasoning, brown sugar, and salt and pepper to taste. Place on the prepared baking sheet. Roast the meat for about 30 minutes, stirring occasionally. Remove from the oven, drain any excess fat, and stir the meat into the tomato sauce.

Add the white beans, bay leaves, parsley, basil, oregano, and the reserved crumbled bacon. Stir to mix well. Top the mixture with the stuffing mix and the thyme leaves. Drizzle the melted butter over the cassoulet. (At this point you can freeze the cassoulet and cook at a later date. It will keep, tightly covered, for about 3 months.)

Place the uncovered Dutch oven in the 425°F oven and cook for 30 minutes. Reduce the heat to 350°F and cook for 30 minutes. With a wooden spoon, break the crust topping and stir into the cassoulet. Bake for another 1 to 1½ hours, breaking the crust topping into the dish every 20 minutes or so. Remove from the oven and let sit for 15 minutes before serving.

NOTE

If the cassoulet seems to dry out during baking, stir in additional beef stock as needed to keep the mixture moist.

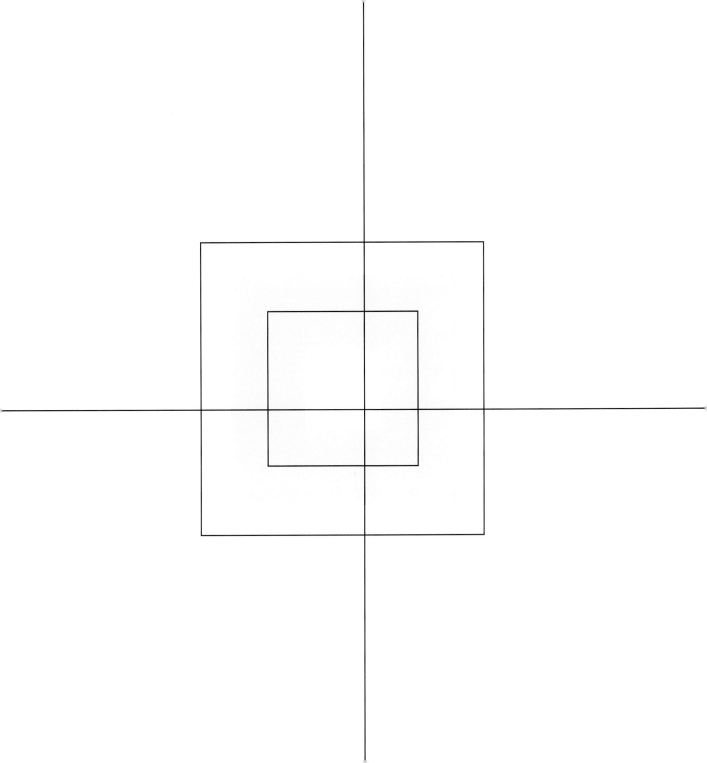

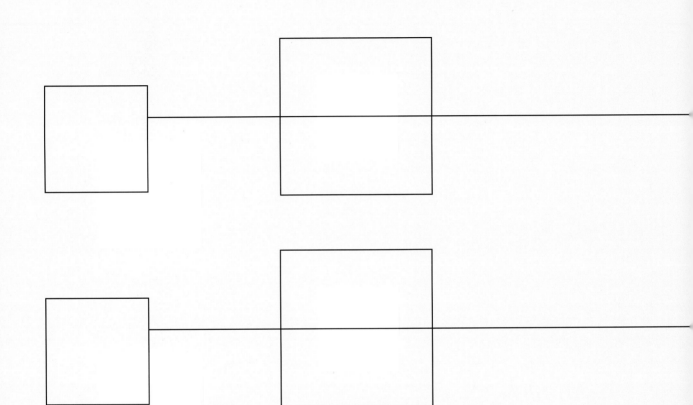

Pasta

FETTUCCINE ALFREDO

MARRAKECH RIGATONI

FARFALLE WITH SPICY SAUSAGE, ARTICHOKES,
AND EXOTIC MUSHROOMS

BRAISED SCALLOPS IN WINE OVER LINGUINE

COMFORTING MACARONI AND CHEESE

FUSILLI WITH TOASTED WALNUT
AND PAN-ROASTED GARLIC SAUCE

CLASSIC PASTA BOLOGNESE

SPAGHETTI ALLA PUTTANESCA

SPAGHETTI WITH TURKEY MEATBALL SAUCE

CHEESE TORTELLINI WITH SMOKED TROUT AND DILL

FETTUCCINE ALFREDO

This is probably my favorite of all the pasta recipes in this book. First of all, it is so simple and easy to make. It's one of those dishes I consider a "pantry staple," meaning I always keep its ingredients on hand for a quick weeknight supper or an impromptu Saturday night gathering of friends. This Fettuccine Alfredo is even better topped with grilled chicken strips, salmon, or shrimp.

SERVES 4 TO 6

2 tablespoons olive oil
3 garlic cloves, chopped
2 tablespoons all-purpose flour
3 cups milk
1 (8 ounce) package cream cheese, cubed and softened

3 cups freshly grated Parmesan cheese, divided
1 (16 ounce) package fettuccine, cooked according to package directions and drained
2 tablespoons chopped fresh parsley
Freshly ground black pepper

In a 5½-quart Dutch oven set over low heat, heat the olive oil until hot. Add the garlic and cook, stirring constantly, for about 2 minutes, being careful not to allow the garlic to brown.

Stir in the flour and cook for 1 minute more. Gradually add the milk, whisking until thoroughly blended.

Raise the heat to medium and cook for about 8 minutes, or until the mixture is thick and bubbly. Stir in the cream cheese and cook for 2 minutes, or until the mixture is smooth and creamy. Add 2½ cups of the Parmesan cheese and stir constantly until the cheese melts.

Remove from the heat and add the cooked pasta. Toss until the cheese sauce evenly coats the pasta.

Place the fettuccine on a large serving platter and top with the remaining ½ cup of Parmesan cheese, chopped parsley, and pepper. Serve at once.

104

MARRAKECH RIGATONI

The soul of northern African cuisine mingles with the heart of Italian cooking in this unique pasta dish, which balances just the right intensity of sweet, spicy, and sour flavors. To make the dinner complete, I like to serve this pasta with a lavash flat bread and fresh sliced fruit drizzled with honey and rose water. For a vegetarian alternative, omit the lamb.

SERVES 6 TO 8

2 tablespoons olive oil
2 pounds ground lamb
1 red onion, thinly sliced
1 red bell pepper, seeded and thinly sliced
4 garlic cloves, chopped
1 medium eggplant, cut into ¾-inch dice
1 (28 ounce) can crushed tomatoes
   with added purée
1 cup red wine
¼ cup apple cider vinegar
2 tablespoons chopped ginger
3 tablespoons chopped fresh mint
2 tablespoons chopped fresh rosemary

1 tablespoon ground cumin
¼ to ½ teaspoon cayenne pepper
½ teaspoon ground cinnamon
1 tablespoon sugar
Salt and freshly ground black pepper
1 (16 ounce) package rigatoni or penne pasta,
   cooked according to package directions
   and drained
1 (15½ ounce) can chickpeas, rinsed and drained
1 cup golden raisins
1 cup pitted green olives, rinsed, drained,
   and sliced
¼ cup capers, rinsed and drained
1 cup feta cheese, crumbled

In a 5½-quart Dutch oven heat the olive oil over medium heat until very hot. Add the lamb, red onion, red pepper, garlic, and eggplant. Cook over medium heat for 10 minutes, stirring often, until the lamb is browned and the vegetables are soft. Drain and discard any excess fat.

Add the crushed tomatoes, red wine, cider vinegar, ginger, mint, rosemary, cumin, cayenne pepper, cinnamon, sugar, and salt and pepper to taste. Cover and reduce the heat to low. Simmer, stirring occasionally, for 45 minutes to 1 hour. Stir in the cooked pasta, chickpeas, raisins, green olives, and capers. Preheat the oven to 400°F. Top the pasta with feta cheese. Place in the oven and bake for about 20 minutes, or until the cheese just begins to melt and the top of the pasta begins to brown slightly. Let sit for 10 minutes before serving.

FARFALLE WITH SPICY SAUSAGE, ARTICHOKES, AND EXOTIC MUSHROOMS

SERVES 6 TO 8

2 ounces exotic dried mushrooms

2 cups red wine

1 pound hot Italian sausage (in casings)

5 tablespoons butter, divided

2 tablespoons olive oil

1 cup fresh sage leaves

1 red onion, thinly sliced

2 red bell peppers, seeded and thinly sliced

4 garlic cloves, chopped

1 (16 ounce) jar marinated artichoke hearts, drained and cut in halves

1 cup beef stock

¼ cup balsamic vinegar

16 ounces farfalle or other short-shaped pasta, cooked according to package directions and drained

¼ cup chopped fresh basil

1 cup grated Parmesan cheese

Salt and freshly ground black pepper

In a large bowl soak the dried mushrooms with the red wine for 1 hour. Drain the mushrooms and set aside. Pour the red wine through a sieve lined with cheesecloth. Measure out 1 cup of the red wine and set aside.

In a 4½-quart Dutch oven barely cover the sausage with cold water, bring the water to a boil, cover, and cook the sausage for 7 to 10 minutes, or until cooked through. Drain and let the sausage cool slightly, then cut into ½-inch slices. With a paper towel dry the inside of the Dutch oven.

In the same Dutch oven, melt 4 tablespoons of the butter with the olive oil. Add the sage leaves and cook over moderately high heat, stirring once or twice, until the leaves are crisp. Remove with a slotted spoon and drain on paper towels.

Add the remaining 1 tablespoon butter to the Dutch oven. Stir in the red onion, red bell pepper, garlic, and mushrooms. Cook until the onions and peppers just begin to wilt, about 7 minutes. Add the artichoke hearts, beef stock, reserved red wine, and balsamic vinegar. Cook over high heat until the liquid is reduced to 1 cup, about 5 to 7 minutes.

Add the farfalle, cooked sausage, basil, and Parmesan cheese. Toss to coat evenly with the sauce. Season to taste with salt and pepper. Transfer the pasta to a large serving bowl and scatter the crisp sage leaves on top. Serve at once.

BRAISED SCALLOPS IN WINE OVER LINGUINE

This pasta comes together in about 15 minutes, so it is a favorite of mine during the summer months in East Hampton, where the long evenings are devoted to browsing village antiques stores, not cooking or entertaining. Fresh scallops should be plump, firm to the touch, and have only the slightest briny smell, like that of the ocean surf. Serve this with a good Italian loaf to dip into the incredible garlicky sauce.

SERVES 6

2 pounds sea scallops, rinsed and drained
Salt and freshly ground black pepper
½ cup olive oil
8 garlic cloves, chopped
½ to 1 teaspoon red pepper flakes
½ cup chopped fresh parsley
1 cup white wine

1 (16 ounce) package linguine, cooked according to package directions and drained
6 plum tomatoes, seeded and coarsely chopped
½ cup thinly sliced fresh basil leaves

Spread the scallops out on a paper towel and blot dry with another towel. Season with salt and pepper. Cut any large scallops in half or quarters if desired. Set aside.

In a 4½-quart Dutch oven heat the oil over medium heat until hot. Add the garlic, red pepper flakes, and parsley. Cook, stirring constantly, for 1 minute.

Add the scallops and quickly sauté, turning as needed, until the scallops just begin to cook, about 1 minute. Add the wine, cover, and bring to a boil. Reduce the heat and allow the scallops to steam for 2 to 3 minutes, or until they are opaque and cooked through.

Place the cooked linguine on a large serving platter. Pour the scallops and wine over the pasta and sprinkle with chopped tomatoes and slivers of basil. Season to taste with salt and pepper. Serve at once.

COMFORTING MACARONI AND CHEESE

This is the classic creamy, cheesy casserole, but I've also included some yummy variations.

SERVES 6

8 tablespoons (1 stick) butter
½ cup all-purpose flour
Salt and freshly ground black pepper
1 tablespoon Dijon-style mustard
2 teaspoons Worcestershire sauce

3 cups milk
4 cups grated cheddar cheese, divided
1 (16 ounce) package elbow macaroni, cooked according to package directions and drained
1 cup seasoned bread crumbs

Preheat the oven to 350°F.

In a 4½-quart Dutch oven melt the butter over medium heat. Add the flour and a sprinkling of salt and pepper. Cook for 2 minutes, stirring constantly, until the mixture is smooth and the color of light straw. Add the Dijon mustard, Worcestershire sauce, and milk. Bring to a boil and cook, uncovered, for 5 minutes, or until thick and bubbly.

Remove from the heat and add 3 cups of the cheddar cheese in handfuls, stirring after each addition until the cheese is melted and smooth. Stir in the cooked macaroni. Top with the remaining 1 cup of cheddar cheese and seasoned bread crumbs.

Cover and bake in the oven until bubbly and heated through, about 30 minutes. Remove the cover and bake for 10 minutes longer to crisp the top of the casserole. Serve at once.

VARIATIONS

- Use grated Swiss, Gruyère, Monterey Jack, or smoked mozzarella cheese in place of the cheddar.
- Add 2 to 3 cups diced, cooked ham or turkey when you stir in the macaroni.
- Add ½ cup chopped, oil-packed sun-dried tomatoes, ½ cup sliced Greek black olives, and 1 cup chopped, marinated artichoke hearts when you stir in the macaroni.
- Add 3 roasted red bell peppers (peeled, seeded, and thinly sliced), 4 ounces thinly sliced smoked salmon, and 2 tablespoons rinsed capers when you stir in the macaroni.
- Add 1 (15½ ounce) can rinsed and drained black beans, ½ cup chopped fresh cilantro, 2 jalapeño peppers (seeded and chopped), and 1 tablespoon chili powder when you stir in the macaroni.

FUSILLI WITH TOASTED WALNUT AND PAN-ROASTED GARLIC SAUCE

SERVES 6

1 tablespoon walnut oil
1 tablespoon olive oil
1 onion, chopped
6 garlic cloves, chopped
2 teaspoons Worcestershire sauce
2½ cups chopped walnuts, pecans,
  or hazelnuts, toasted and cooled (see note)
½ cup white wine
½ teaspoon saffron threads, crumbled
1½ cups heavy cream

1½ cups freshly grated Parmesan cheese, divided
1 (16 ounce) package fusilli or other short-
  shape pasta, cooked according to package
  directions and drained
Salt and freshly ground black pepper
3 green onions, chopped
2 tablespoons chopped fresh parsley

In a 5½-quart Dutch oven heat the walnut oil and the olive oil over medium-high heat until sizzling. Add the onion and garlic, reduce the heat to medium, and cook for 6 to 8 minutes, or until the onions just begin to brown.

Transfer this mixture to a food processor. Add the Worcestershire sauce, 2 cups of the toasted nuts, white wine, saffron threads, and heavy cream. Process until smooth.

Pour the sauce back into the Dutch oven and heat to a simmer. Cook for 3 minutes, stirring constantly. Remove from the heat and stir in 1 cup of the Parmesan cheese. Add the cooked pasta and toss to coat completely.

Place the tossed pasta on a large serving platter. Season to taste with salt and pepper. Sprinkle the remaining Parmesan cheese, green onions, parsley, and remaining chopped nuts on top. Serve at once.

NOTE
To toast nuts, preheat the oven to 350°F. Place the nuts on a baking sheet and toast, stirring occasionally, for 5 to 8 minutes, or until the nuts are lightly browned and aromatic.

110

CLASSIC PASTA BOLOGNESE

Other than a subtle grating of fresh nutmeg, no additional herbs or spices are added to this simple, rich sauce. Instead, this classic bolognese derives its flavor from the very slow cooking of the meat and vegetables in the wine and milk.

SERVES 6

4 tablespoons butter

¼ cup olive oil

2 onions, chopped

3 carrots, diced

2 ribs of celery, diced

3 pounds very coarsely ground chuck or round steak (not hamburger meat)*

Salt and freshly ground black pepper

1½ cups white wine

1 cup half and half or milk

Freshly grated nutmeg

2 (28 ounce) cans chopped tomatoes with their juice

1 (16 ounce) package spaghetti, fettuccine, or tagliatelle, cooked according to package directions and drained

1 cup freshly grated Parmesan cheese

* Have your butcher very coarsely grind the beef for you.
Hamburger meat is too finely ground and does not work well in this recipe.

In a 5½-quart Dutch oven melt the butter with the olive oil over medium heat. Add the onions, carrots, and celery. Cook until the onion softens, about 5 minutes. Add the beef and cook, breaking up the meat with a spoon, until the meat is just brown. Lightly season with salt and pepper.

Add the white wine and cook over medium-high heat until all the liquid has evaporated, about 5 to 8 minutes. Be sure to stir continually so that the sauce does not scorch. Add the half and half or milk and a generous sprinkling of freshly grated nutmeg. Continue cooking over medium-high heat until the milk has evaporated. Stir in the chopped tomatoes with their juice. When the sauce begins to bubble, reduce the heat to a very low simmer.

Cook, uncovered, for 3 hours, stirring occasionally, until the bolognese is very thick and flavorful. Stir in the cooked pasta and freshly grated Parmesan cheese. Toss to coat evenly. Cover and remove from the heat. Let sit for 5 minutes to allow the pasta to absorb the sauce. Serve at once.

SPAGHETTI ALLA PUTTANESCA

I call this spicy dish one of my "pantry pastas," since I usually have all of the ingredients on hand and can make the recipe in less than 30 minutes. You can make the dish hotter by adding more red pepper. Puttanesca translates to "whore's sauce" and was a quick means of nourishment for a busy "working girl."

SERVES 6

⅓ cup olive oil

12 anchovy fillets

6 garlic cloves, chopped

½ teaspoon red pepper flakes
   (or more to taste)

Salt

1 (28 ounce) can crushed tomatoes
   with added purée

48 brine-cured black olives, rinsed, pitted,
   and halved

3 tablespoons capers, rinsed and drained

1 (16 ounce) package spaghetti, cooked
   according to package directions and drained

1 cup coarsely chopped flat-leaf parsley

In a 5½-quart Dutch oven combine the olive oil, anchovies, garlic, red pepper flakes, and salt to taste. Cook over medium heat until the garlic turns golden but does not brown, about 2 to 3 minutes. Stir in the tomatoes, olives, and capers. Reduce the heat to medium-low and simmer, uncovered, for 15 to 20 minutes, or until sauce has thickened.

Add the spaghetti and toss to coat. Cover and remove from the heat. Let sit for 5 minutes to allow the pasta to absorb some of the sauce. Stir in the chopped parsley and serve immediately.

112

SPAGHETTI WITH TURKEY MEATBALL SAUCE

2 pounds very lean ground turkey
1 onion, finely chopped
8 garlic cloves, finely chopped, divided
1 green bell pepper, seeded and finely chopped
2 eggs, lightly beaten
⅔ cup seasoned bread crumbs
2 tablespoons chopped fresh basil
1 tablespoon chopped fresh oregano
1 tablespoon chopped fresh rosemary
1 to 2 teaspoons fennel seeds, crushed
Salt and freshly ground black pepper
¼ cup olive oil

1 onion, chopped
2 carrots, chopped
2 ribs of celery, chopped
2 tablespoons all-purpose flour
1½ cups chicken stock
¼ cup balsamic vinegar
1 (28 ounce) can crushed tomatoes
    with added purée
1 to 2 tablespoons dried Italian seasoning
2 teaspoons sugar
1 (16 ounce) package spaghetti, cooked
    according to package directions and drained
1 cup grated Parmesan cheese

In a large bowl combine the ground turkey, finely chopped onion, half of the chopped garlic, green bell pepper, eggs, bread crumbs, basil, oregano, rosemary, fennel seeds, and salt and pepper to taste. Shape the mixture into 1½- inch meatballs and place them on a baking sheet that has been lined with parchment paper. Cover and refrigerate for 30 minutes.

In a 5½-quart Dutch oven heat the olive oil until hot over medium-high heat. Add the turkey meatballs in batches and brown on all sides, about 3 to 4 minutes. With a slotted spoon remove the meatballs to a plate lined with paper towels and drain.

Discard all but 3 tablespoons of the drippings in the Dutch oven. Add the chopped onion, carrots, the remaining chopped garlic, and celery. Cook until lightly browned, about 10 minutes. Stir in the flour and cook for 3 minutes. Add the chicken stock, balsamic vinegar, crushed tomatoes, Italian seasoning, sugar and salt and pepper to taste. Simmer, uncovered, stirring occasionally to prevent sticking, for 30 minutes.

Add the meatballs. Cook, stirring gently so as not to break up the meatballs, for another 30 minutes, or until the sauce is very thick.

Place the cooked spaghetti on a large serving platter. Generously ladle the meatball sauce over the hot pasta and sprinkle with grated Parmesan cheese before serving.

CHEESE TORTELLINI WITH SMOKED TROUT AND DILL

This recipe relies on fresh store-bought tortellini to make it quick and easy. For a variation, substitute thinly sliced prosciutto ham for the smoked trout and fresh basil for the dill. Omit the capers and add pine nuts in their place. Garnish with fresh sprigs of basil.

SERVES 4

2 tablespoons olive oil

2 red onions, thinly sliced

1 red bell pepper, seeded and cut into thin strips

1 (28 ounce) can diced tomatoes with their juice

1 cup heavy cream

1½ cups grated Romano or Parmesan cheese, divided

3 tablespoons vodka

⅓ cup chopped fresh dill

½ pound smoked trout or salmon, cut into bite-sized pieces

3 tablespoons capers, rinsed and drained

2 tablespoons fresh lemon juice

½ (10 ounce) package prewashed spinach, stems removed

1 (16 ounce) package fresh cheese-filled tortellini pasta, cooked according to package directions and drained

Salt and freshly ground black pepper

Fresh dill sprigs

Lemon wedges

In a 5½-quart Dutch oven heat the olive oil over medium-high heat. Add the red onion and red bell pepper and cook until crisp-tender, about 3 minutes. Add the diced tomatoes and cook, uncovered, for 15 minutes, or until the sauce is thick and slightly reduced.

Stir in the heavy cream, 1 cup of the cheese, and vodka. Cook, uncovered, for 5 minutes, or until the cheese is melted and smooth.

Add the chopped dill, smoked trout, capers, and lemon juice. Gently stir in the spinach and cooked tortellini. Season to taste with salt and pepper. Cover, remove from the heat, and let sit 5 minutes to allow the pasta to absorb some of the sauce and the spinach leaves to wilt.

Transfer to a serving platter. Sprinkle the pasta with the remaining cheese. Garnish with fresh dill sprigs and lemon wedges. Serve at once.

This book is a collaborative effort. I may be in the forefront but there are many others behind me, making it all possible.

I gratefully acknowledge my parents, Jan and Ray Overton, for their wisdom and guidance. Thank you to my brother, Ricky, my sister, Robyn, her husband, Tim, and my nieces, Hope and Emma, for their constant support and enthusiasm. I am grateful to my grandmother, Granny Lou, who first introduced me to the kitchen. And I can't forget my little four-legged "kids," my West Highland terriers, Gypsy and Cagney, for their total devotion and morning kisses. (They think I'm the best.) You all help to make me whole.

Thank you to Nathalie Dupree for teaching me and showing me the way to enjoy a successful culinary career.

Thank you to my assistant, Susan Montgomery, for making my job such a joy. And for your lasting friendship.

To my editor, Suzanne De Galan, thank you for making sense of my words and for your devotion to making all my projects a success, for your good common-sense, your comforting manner, and general hand-holding to the end. I love and appreciate you more than you know. To Burtch Hunter, who has conceived the look of my last three cookbooks, who could ask for a better friend or more talented designer. I am in awe of your talents. To Sherry Wade, a tireless associate editor (whom I can always get on the phone), thanks for your dedication and determination to meet deadlines. And for your smile. Special thanks to Melanie Lasoff for seeing this project through to completion. To Scott Bard, Amy Burton, and Robyn Richardson, thank you for your excellent promotional efforts. And special thanks, once again, to Chuck Perry, Steve Gracie, and Marge McDonald for giving me my literary start and for continuing to support my endeavors.

Thank you to Brad Newton, my photographer, who was able to capture the essence and feel of this book with his inspired images, and to his assistant, Parker C. Smith, for making the photo sessions flow. I especially appreciate my prop and food stylist, Lynne Mitchell. Your talent and eye for detail are apparent in every photograph. Thank you to styling assistant Winnifer Chih Kuang for helping Lynne achieve that goal. Special thanks to the folks at Williams-Sonoma for the use of many of the props used in the pictures. And again, heartfelt thanks to Vicky Murphy, Jim Laber, and Chris Rosenberger of Inland Seafood in Atlanta for providing the freshest and the best seafood available for the photographs, and for some of the recipe testing in this book.

The pictures would not have been possible without some behind-the-scenes preparation from dedicated friends and co-workers Susan Montgomery, Carolyn Packard, Jane Fasse, and Michele Phillips. Thank you too, Michele, for assisting me at the shoot itself. It made my life so much easier.

I am grateful to Finn Schjorring and Faye Gooding of Le Creuset of America, Inc. for their constant support of my school and book projects. And to Monique Gainsley, Wade Hyde, David Duvall, Barbara Fogle, and Laura Gabbard for helping to make Ray Overton's Le Creuset Cooking School in Atlanta, the source of these recipes, a place of enjoyment and education.

I want to thank my friends (and food "guinea pigs") Kay Ponder, Nancy McKenna, Jeff Eisenberg, Brian Seifried, Stephen Barnwell, Ken Folds, Clint Bearden, Allan Vineyard, Donald Alexander, Heyward Young, Kenny Conley, Virginia Willis, Will Deller, and Nancy Rogers. In your own ways, you all make my life fun and content.

And finally, thank you to all the many unnamed apprentices who work so diligently to help make my classes fun and rewarding, and to the nearly 10,000 students I have been able to teach and entertain over the years. Your desire to learn and devoted enthusiasm helped make *Dutch Oven Cooking* a reality.

Child, Julia. *The Way to Cook*. New York: Alfred A. Knopf, 1989.

Choate, Judith. *The Bean Cookbook*. New York: Kenan Books, 1992.

Corriher, Shirley O. *CookWise: The Hows and Whys of Cooking Revealed*. New York: William Morrow and Company, 1997.

Cutler, Carol. *Catch of the Day*. Mount Vernon, NY: Consumers Union of United States, 1990.

Dupree, Nathalie. *Nathalie Dupree Cooks for Family and Friends*. New York: William Morrow and Company, Inc., 1991.

_____. *Nathalie Dupree's Southern Memories*. New York: Crown Publishing Group, 1993.

Ferrary, Jeanette and Fiszer, Louise. *Sweet Onions & Sour Cherries*. New York: Simon & Schuster, 1992.

Fobel, Jim. *Jim Fobel's Big Flavors*. New York: Crown Publishing Group, 1995.

Fong-Torres, Shirley. *In the Chinese Kitchen with Shirley Fong-Torres*. Berkeley, CA: Pacific View Press, 1993.

Herbst, Sharon Tyler. *New Food Lover's Companion*. New York: Barron's Educational Series, 1995.

Kimball, Christopher. *The Cook's Bible: The Best of American Home Cooking*. Boston: Little, Brown and Company, 1996.

Loomis, Susan Herrman. *The Great American Seafood Cookbook*. New York: Workman Publishing, 1988.

McGee, Harold. *On Food and Cooking: The Science and Lore of the Kitchen*. New York: Scribner's Publishing, 1984.

Miller, Mark. *Coyote Cafe*. Berkeley, CA: Ten Speed Press, 1989.

_____. *The Great Chile Book*. Berkeley, CA: Ten Speed Press, 1991.

Montague, Prosper. *New Larousse Gastronomique*. Twickenham, England: Hamlyn, 1960.

O'Neill, Molly. *New York Cookbook*. New York: Workman Publishing, 1992.

Prudhomme, Paul. *Chef Paul Prudhomme's Louisiana Kitchen*. New York: William Morrow and Company, 1984.

Rogers, Mara Reid. *The South The Beautiful Cookbook*. San Francisco: Collins Publishers, 1996.

Schmidt, Stephen. *Master Recipes*. New York: Fawcett Columbine Books, 1987.

Southern Living Staff. *The Southern Living Cookbook*. Birmingham, AL: Oxmoor House, 1987.

Spear, Ruth. *The East Hampton Cookbook of Menus and Recipes*. New York: Dell Publishing, 1975.

Wells, Patricia. *Trattoria*. New York: William Morrow and Company, 1993.

Willan, Anne. *La Varenne Pratique: The Complete Illustrated Guide to the Techniques, Ingredients and Tools of Classic Modern Cooking*. New York: Crown Publishing Group, 1989.

Wolfert, Paula. *The Cooking of the Eastern Mediterranean*. New York: HarperCollins Publishers, 1994.